Last Wave
A Poem Journal

poems by

Philip Comfort

Finishing Line Press
Georgetown, Kentucky

Last Wave
A Poem Journal

Publisher: Leah Huete de Maines
Editor: Christen Kincaid
Author Photo: Philip Comfort
Cover Design: Elizabeth Maines McCleavy

Order online: www.finishinglinepress.com
          also available on amazon.com

Author inquiries and mail orders:
Finishing Line Press
P. O. Box 1626
Georgetown, Kentucky 40324
U. S. A.

A tribute to Georgia, my wife, in memoriam

All week long they kept coming like waves—
friends and the beloved family of Georgia
grieving and weeping, knowing this would be
the last time they would see her—
then, as her days got shorter in the winter sun
we watched her breathe in agony,
her heart pounding its last beats,
until she expired her gentle breath,
and we raised our hands in praise
to the Lord, thanking him for taking her
into his glorious sunset presence—
the spirit of Georgia leaving her body
mingled with the sacred Spirit of God
rushing through us, rising like dawn,
as she passed into heaven, transcending earth,
visiting many souls on the way to Paradise
while the glorious Spirit of God lingered with us
as her lifeless body was lying on the deathbed,
I saw a beautiful woman
who used to walk on music like water
who used to turn the ordinary into miracles
who always breathed the wonderful Spirit of God
who once spirited to the other side,
where she saw the spirit of her great grandmother,
who, every night, thanked her celestials
and deceased friends, whom she called "all y'all."
She lived the better part of the Bible,
incarnating love and amazing grace—
she cared for the poor, befriended the lonely,
she became a member of the Wacamma tribe.
Georgia loved to pray to the Spirit of Jesus,
never doubting he would take her to Heaven,
where her friends and departed family members
waited to see her in glory and receive her in peace—
for, as always she said, "the earth is a good place to leave"
I loved her, I love her and I cherish her.
I will live on until I hear her make music again—
until then, like an angel, she watches over her many friends.
I dedicate this book to her.

Tom Anastasis, a fifty-five year-old widower, is diagnosed with pancreatic cancer. Foregoing treatment, he decides to go to an island in the Caribbean, and spend his last days there—although he secretly hopes he might be miraculously healed. So he told his adult sons he would be gone for three or four months, and not to worry about him. He had taken up writing poetry and decided to write a poem journal. Throughout the journal he uses the personal "I" and speaks in the present tense. (He usually writes the poem journal every night before he sleeps.) If he does live, he wants to give the journal to his sons. If he doesn't, he hopes they can read it after he is gone.

He navigates a small boat to get there (which he keeps upright all the time on the island to catch rainwater), and he brings along fishing gear (nets, hooks, lines, spear, etc.), 20 gallon bottles of water, a shovel, other necessities, and a small outdoor stove. He sets up a tarp on the sand attached to his boat— like a lean-two—for shelter. He takes his golden retriever, Luke, with him. The dog is very old and might not live much longer. He brings his snorkeling gear, and longboard for surfing—as best as he can at his age (he can surf two-to-four footers with a back brace—they are call "old man's waves"). At first, he is able to surf, then it gets more painful, and then he can't surf at all. He enjoys sunrises on the eastern side of the island (the Atlantic Ocean—with a reef one hundred yards out) and sunsets on the western side (the Caribbean Sea), the rolling sea, the winging seabirds, and a pod of intelligent dolphins, who become his friends. He also befriends a fox.

As Tom searches for God in the natural world of sea, sunrise, and sunset, he experiences the divine Spirit in wonderful ways, and he realizes his connectedness with all living things. Tom becomes accustomed to the daily, constant rhythm of the moving tide, the flowing waves, the movement of sunrise, zenith, and sunset, moon-rise and moon-set, the changing color and texture of the clouds, the lack of rain and the falling of rain. All this movement is reflected in the poems.

Tom is an existentialist Jesus-follower, who has been influenced especially by the living Spirit of Jesus, Native American spirituality, and somewhat by Buddhist spirituality. He views his entire time on the island as a vision quest. Though he hopes for a miraculous healing, he understands that life is a journey and that his exodus from earth most likely will come shortly— when he will be set free from his body to join the spirit-world of the Great Mystery. He struggles with his mortality and wonders if he should just swim out into the sea and die, or wait for death to take him. He receives many visions from the beyond—visions from God about the meaning of life and the afterlife.

As in agonizing childbirth, the cosmos was born in pain. The planets around our sun had a tumultuous beginning; the moon erupted from earth, planets collided, and our seas were created by violent cosmic bombardments. Even now, as Tom watches the turbulent waves, he knows beauty rises from destruction, and resplendence shines from an orb that's burning itself to death; yet in the midst of this oblivion, flocks of seabirds soar, dolphins porpoise, whales breach, stingrays rocket into air, and humans can know that in their last hour they need not despair because death is a beginning and God is the Lord of the living. Death is not a failure; dying without God is.

Day One

I know where they come from.
I have seen them many times
(each wave, a man's life).
but never in their beginnings—
when the **black** winds Yowl on $_{abyssal}$ seas—
ebony **black**, African **black** gusts, brutal **black** squalls,
sable gales, **dark** blusters stirring *whirls and whorls,*
heaving benthic brine into swelling energy,
as storms unleash **fury** on white-capped seas,
and give painful birth to swollen surf,
where swells peel off in symmetrical form—
ominous lumps fetching miles from shore,
lumbering beasts advancing in feral splendor
heading toward shallow **rugged** shoals,
where oceanic clash forces the swell $^{to\ rise.}$
this is where I have seen them—
when they ^{jump} crazily in size,
rounding, shaping, and curling water
billowing beautifully brutal,
water rushing back up the face,
forming a barrel perfectly shaped,
where time suspends and spirit transcends
as the wave $^{hangs\ in\ the\ sky—}$
its crest feathering flowing spindrifts—
dawning *light* shooting through the tube,
surreal, chimerical, ethereal,
crystalline *light*, cherubim bright—
the wave hovering for an eternal moment
just before $^{the\ peak}$ cascades and $_{falls}$
clanging on $_{the\ trough}$ like a pair of cymbals
(the percussion having gotten closer and louder),
the lip landing with a **whomping crescendo**
in a *wild-white-water* explosion
rushing to shore like stallions stampeding—
galloping ghosts of froth and foam,
sea spraying *bent* sky and $^{rising\ sun—}$
and then I see another one and another one!
how many more will come?

Day Two

as I walk the shore with Luke, my golden retriever,
tireless sea keeps *breaking* toward me,
rushing to me, *flowing* to me, *running* to me, *rolling* to me—
beachcomber, breAkeR, beachcomber, bReaKer—
God coming, God coming, God never gone.

a super-strong southern wind sweeps the seashore.
waves whitecap, sand leaps and somersaults;
the deep and shallow are alive with verve,
calling me to swim the beachcombers and brine—
rushing, thumping waves penetrate my ears;
liquid thrust pounds me, foam surrounds me.
I am knocked over by the force of fury.
my dog paddles like *crazy* to keep his head ^{above the water.}
I surface, gasp for breath, suck in sea,
am pummeled again, then again, then again—
the ocean-Spirit is as violent as she is kind.

when I get out of the water, I watch a flock of pelicans
disappear into the long *t h i n* u n r e a c h a b l e horizon.
(I am *wet with color, drenched in sun.*)
I see sea-spirit ^{rise with sun}, ink *light*, speak wind.
(I have read a thousand pages.)
sea-spirited, unveiled, epiphanic faces
ghost into water, spirit into waves.
(I chase a multitude of memories—
as sea ghosts crash into lacey froth,
billow and trough, heave and slough.)*

the spirit is wind, the spirit is ocean;
waves of wildebeests *stampede* the horizon,
flocks of migratory aviaries paddle ^{the sky.}
I see their *sun-strewn* **shadows** *wing* across the shore.
I hear the percussing breakers **beat** the littoral,
as I paddle my surfboard deeper into the wake,
waiting for the waves to form and break—
catching sleek rollers flowing to the right and left,

as my mind mushes into spiritual liquid,
and I become sea, surf, wind, and spirit.

Day Three

I am awakened in the morning, fall back asleep, and have a dream
about the beginning where **darkness** swarmed the face of the **deep**—
theophanic *phantoms* covered sky, sea, and shore.
the Spirit moved mightily, ^{brooding over} the ocean waters
until life was conceived and formed in the sea's placenta—
every living moving creature was born of her—
the sea anemones, the jelly fish, the squids, the sharks,
the sea turtles, the dolphins, the marlins, and the whales.

the cerulean ocean is my womb and tomb—
I come from her (my genesis) and go to her (my apocalypse)
I dive into the heaving sea, accepting my destiny,
as I swim with the dolphins ^{emerging} and _{submerging}

Day Four

as Luke (my dog) and I walk, I gaze out at the ocean's horizon—
the sea is still, and so is the *sun,* as I in-breathe
"is-ness"— the essence of quintessence
the zen of being—not doing anything
(silent, serene breathing)
and "now-ness"—was, is, will be, at once
this moment ever born again and again
never dying—the I AM that I AM
and "with-ness"— God's present presence
given by grace, discovered in God's face

silver cloud-smeared horizon
where sea and sky touch
a slim slit reveals partial *sun*
casting a *beam* on the rippling seas
following me wherever I step

ubiquitous wind in ^{bird-flight}
drenched seashore, soused sea,
the coast, a wet sponge, drips divinity—
I walk the beach smothered by the Almighty
and admire the giving-and-forgiving waves
always replenished by another one

the sky cleansed by the sun is another poem
the sea is broken-open scripture
to be read until the sun dies down

Day Five

super ^{sunrise-}streaks *rip* through the white flimsy clouds
cerulean ocean spreads on the littoral like watercolor paint
lapping the shore with more than a thousand gallons of blue

I spot the backs of two whales (mother and calf) headed north—
spouting surreal, lingering in the Atlantic waters
breeching boldly into the bald spring air
where I can see their flukes and light gray bellies—
these leviathans ^{suspending midway} between earth and sky
are the leviathans God breathes into being,
whose divine design drives them to keep on diving
into the _{depths} of the _{abyss} in search of fish

when they ^{emerge} I am resurrected into *light*
and understand the miracle of mammals in the sea
needing air as much as God, as much as the Spirit of life

Day Six

corona ^{rises} over the vanishing horizon . . .
waves muscle their way ^{over} the reef—
revelations of God-gone-ghost.
watery faces of specters appear,
as zephyrs shape-shift the sea.
seasounds flash *light* in crushed waves;
ancient waters spout forgotten music.
I heave poetry in syn-co-pat-ed breaks.
I offer up a libation of praise.
I watch the wild *sun*-wind ^{hold} up waves and swirling seagulls
(multi-colored as the surf—silver gray, bright white),
who stir ^{above} the ocean crashing earth.

the morning sky is as red (bright red!)
as the head of a pileated woodpecker;
the firmament sleek and smooth,
as a thoroughbred's long neck.
stallion waves canter, then *gallop* to shore;
all the **wild animal** in me runs with them.
my spirit ^{soars} to wonderfully **wild realms**—
I am overwhelmed with espials.

the day dies peacefully—
the blood of the *sun* oozing into the horizon,
the m()()n rising majestically, filling the **black** sky.
the seabirds sleep. I sleep alongside my dog, Luke.
I am lulled by the ceaseless sound of breaking waves—
I dream of God walking on an e n d l e s s shore.

Day Seven

my dog, Luke, and I walk the sea long before *dawn*
when the earth and sky are **black**, charcoal **black**,
livid **black**, ebony **black**, an African mask, bark **black**,
crow **black**, dead **black**, blackbird **black**,
forest black, bible black, priest's garb **black**,
blacker than a cat could see,
blacker than Satan could make me believe;
deep hole **black**, deepest hole **black**,
with no sign of the next shovelful turning over anything but **black**.
everything is obsidian, **blackness** heavier than water;
it is poor **black**, worn-out **black**, old tar and tire-tread **black**,
slow **black**, very slow **black**.
then it turns gray a bit like the tip of lit charcoal,
the ash of a cigarette, the gray of vapid dense fog,
wet gray, gray ghosts of it, pale, ghostly obscure,
cold gray, old battleship gray, Icelandic autumn gray,
dilapidated tombstones gray, civil war monuments gray,
Cape Cod gray, worn roads tarred long ago—
I don't know if this gray is better than the **black**.
I just want the *sun* to color the waves, the beach, the air.

like an egg broken on the horizon,
the *sun* is a feast for my eyes;
the sea, rippled like ribs, is sumptuous fare—
I inhale ocean air, in-breathe morning mana.

my day begins with prayer
(to the four winds of the universe),
as the *sun* breaches the horizon,
then s l o w l y turns banana yellow,
looking like a rounded bunch of fruit—
some invisible branch holding the stem.
I dine on the $^{sun\text{-}sea\text{-}rising}$ and breathe thalassic uprooting—
the $_{deep}$ coming to the surface;
the $_{abyss}$ becoming God's face, *which I silently surf across.*

10

the *sun* _{sets} and evening begins.
in deep dark of night Sirius *shines bright,*
Proxima Centauri *glistens and beams—*
could an earth-like planet be orbiting
a sun-like star somewhere in our galaxy?

Day Eight

once *dawn* comes, off-shore winds
hold ^{up} the r o l l i n g beachcombers
and the *swift* pelicans surfing them.
I throw bits of fish to the seagulls who,
like acrobats, snatch them mid-air—
then scavenging **blackbirds** appear.

aviaries are not only *artists* and *poets*,
they wing me into ^{space} like *astronauts*.

as I gambol in the littoral,
running like a child into the rolling sea—
waves knock me around and down,
ocean floods my nose and ears.
what uncontrollable laughter!
what pure nascent joy!
as Luke and I lope in the rushing shallows—
I in God, and God in me—
a mingling of the Wavemaker with my spirit,
freed to frolic in the crush and foam like a dolphin porpoising,
like a seabird flinging wings into the *sun*-broken sky—
I body-surf a roller in the incoming tide.
my dog, Luke, rides the same wave.

wind on waves orchestrates—
percussion, piano, woodwinds, strings—
the music of the sea is my poetry.

then phantoms of fog shroud the island.
I can see only the luminosity of *breaking* waves.
for all I know there is only Spirit ^{hovering} on the coast like seagulls,
smothering me in Ghost—I *walk the shore baptized in voices,*
as fog, thick as God, envelopes the island,
soaks the coast, souses the sea-air,
spray-paints the sky a hundred shades of gray—
I hear—but cannot see—cawing seagulls ^{overhead}
and believe in the parousia of the sun

Day Nine

dark winds scrub **black** ocean.
breaking waves, the only *lumen*—
I *wait for sound to turn to sight.*
the sun ^{ascends and bobbles} on the sea,
and ^{the firmament} flashes with flight
as I watch distant specks soar into SIZE:
volant cormorants speed in V-formation,
pelicans sky-surf *bright* undulations
above the waves which are constantly praying

as I slowly walk in *dawn*, listen to ocean,
and breathe into my spirit universal deity,
I sense there is no difference between myself and sea—
we share the same soul, pneuma, and zoe.
in spirit I am wave-^{rise}-bend-_{break}-crush-*crash.*
I am seabird FlingingWings into wet sky;
in dolphins I porpoise, in me they stride.

sky breathes wind, sea surges,
roaring mountains of waves Avalanche,
tumultuousTumblersTossOcean toward me.
I hear whir of after-crash-crunch, flap-smack of BendingBreak,
incessant RoarFizzleSizzle—I paddle against these relentlessBreakers,
 praying mercy from Omnipresent, Omnipotent SeaMaker.

Day Ten

in the dazzling morning sun-light I see
the ocean's mouth swallowing the seashore
all the beach turns liquid glistening in the *sunlight*—
the tide is thigh-high only a few feet from shore
but still, the far-out waves are breaking bright.
Luke and I paddle out as far as we can go near the reef—
he, keeping his nostrils above the water
me, keeping the nose of the board above the surf—
when we get out to where the waves rise and form,
I can tell he wants to get on my surfboard.
I dismount the board, untie the leash, and help Luke get on—
then I shove him into a breaking wave—he falls off—
so we try again—he catches it and rides all the way to shore—
as I hoot-and-holler-after-him: "go all the way in!"
I retrieve the board, and paddle out and catch a beauty!
we take turns all morning in-the-*sun*-and-sea surfing *glory*!

Day Eleven

the potent m()()n drags ocean's tide again and again
the current shifts, the drift changes from $_{low}$ to ^{high}
all day long—impacting when I fish, swim, and surf—
mid-tide is best for everything—the perfect time
to enter the water or walk the firm-packed sand

today I surf at mid-tide, taking right and left small peaks,
catching the crests at just the right time to glide
down the glacis, to slide down the face of the wave—
feeling the surge in body and soul, enjoying the rush
of a God-*moment*, a Spirit-*flow*, an epiphanic *burst*

Day Twelve

the waves are divine prophets chanting jeremiads,
weeping for the tragedy called human history.
long before mankind subdued earth,
the sun, wind, and sea surged;
and after mankind has destroyed itself,
the *sun*, wind, and sea will still surge.

beauty will not die by the hands of men—
the *sun* will still paint *glorious* h o r i z o n s,
the wind will carry clouds in majestic ^{skies,}
and the waves will form and curl ^{as they rise.}

the sea is greater than my pain.
the *sun* is stronger than my illness.
they will live on, and so will I in spirit.
until then—I surf the *sunlit* ocean,
walk the beach, fish with my spear gun,
drink water from my gallons I brought,
cook and eat fillets with my dog, Luke.

at night I am carried away in spirit in a dream:
I see a vision of all wild animals revived
and alive roaming new earth—
all quadrupeds, bipeds, and winged creatures
filling the world with *zoe*—
I see de-extinct eyes, wings, legs, feet,
hands, heads, mouths, tongues
praising the coming of new earth and heavens.

Day Thirteen

the next morning, *sun*-blasts hammer my head,
torrents of heat melt my face.
I am fried by Helios hell,
as the *sun* screwdrivers my brain with pain
and nails my body to the burning sand.
I seek relief in the cool ocean. Luke and I swim.

in the evening I have a dream-vision—in my revelry
I see the heavens open in another dimension:
the Logos-Spirit is surrounded by myriad angels,
cherubim, seraphim, martyrs, and saints.
the living *zoa* circle him, who has seven eyes
of the seven Spirits sent forth into all the earths.
I see the Logos-Spirit traveling to many worlds in various galaxies.
for each visitation, the Logos-Spirit, assumes a different incarnation.
with many Names, he appears as Redeemer, Liberator, Avatar,
Mediator between all the living creatures and Creator.
he is the Sage and the Savior, the inspirer of myriad books
of Scripture written in thousands of languages.
he has many names, forms, and faces.
in the colossal panegyric assembly, where all his families gather,
he is kind King and awesome Lord.
aquatic creatures from myriad seas swim around him.
aviaries from multiple skies fly above him.
wild quadrupeds prance before him.
anthropic bipeds walk with him.
everywhere are living fins, wings, hooves, feet, and faces.
Hindus realize him as the unique Avatar.
Native Americans worship him as Wakan Tanka,
whose Great Spirit fills the universe like *sunlight* flooding the skies.
Naturalists revere him as nature's Progenitor,
who pervades creation with Spirit and *zoe.*
Taoists know he is the way, the flow.
He is the immortal mortal, the resurrection and the life, the *light of light,*
the everlasting Highest, the ultimate Illuminator, the God of gods,
the Lord of lords, the Prince of princes.
all the sentient creatures praise him,

hail him in whom they live and have their being—
Lord of *suns*, m()()ns, stars, earths, seas, Lord of the living,
Lord of the dead until they're alive again,
Lord of Sheol, Lord of Hades and Paradise, Lord omnipotent,
Lord omnipresent, Lord Spirit, the giver and sustainer of life!
He connects all sentient beings, holding them together as one!

Day Fourteen

in early morning **darkness** I walk under *Venus and Sirius*
(the m()()n is nowhere to be seen);
dark sky is reflected in **deep green** ocean
until it turns *bright* in morning *light.*
waves of seabirds cross the horizon—red knots, marbled godwits,
black skimmers *cruising* southwest where *zephyrs* waft.
then I see another flock ^{lift off} and s c a t t e r l i k e s e e d in the ^{sky}
until they align in V-formation paddling the brisk air to *paradise.*

the morning seagulls on shore are gray and white,
like the fog and sea now rolling in.
phantasmic mist enshrouds the island,
where the dead and alive gather together
(departed ghosts and breathing spirits).
Jesus, Spirit-God, is felt here,
thick in palpable presence, *thin* as air.

thick fog suffusing the island, **dense mist** clouding the ocean—
I can barely see the seagulls soaring south.
then a shaft of *sun* ^{shoots up} the horizon—
the entire east turns *brilliant* orange, as the bright *orb* ascends
and slides behind some clouds again—
the Divine is seen in *beauty* and **darkness.**

I read the l i n e s of the ocean—
the *successive* waves, a speaking poem.
Logos, the primordial spirit-voice,
is ever creating, ever pneumatic—
his entire flowing universe is cymatic:
oscillating spheres roll and unscroll.

the day dies painfully red,
as the _{drop-dead} *sun* bleeds into the western sky.
darkness emerges, as does a bloody m()()n
flooding the western horizon.
I sleep and dream of eternal waves,
^{rising}, forming, cresting, _{spilling} e n d l e s s l y . . .

Day Fifteen

the seaside is spring-warm and pleasant,
when, all-of-a-sudden, a northwestern *blows* in—
cold clouds, **dark** wind and rain *drench* the coast,
brisk waves STIFFEN, the *sun* disappears—
all is eerie green-gray except the white foam
that *splashes and splurges* on the reef—
I am awestruck by the sudden seacoast assault.

on this *sky-fall, rain-drenched, sun-hid* morning,
I look for God among the sea-oats;
I seek his Spirit in the sea-waves
and in the ocean's zephyrs and winds.
the Divine is not far from me.
I look _{under rocks and shells.}
I peer into the gray *heavens*
searching for anything with meaning,
and still it keeps raining.

when the rain stops, I watch a *solo* dolphin porpoise south
and a *lonely* seagull foraging in the littoral
waiting for her only friend—the _{rising sun.}
the closest planet like our rocky earth
is only a few *light-years* away—
and there are numerous others within our galaxy.
it is God who created space and invisible matter
that fills our star-*lit* world and every other—
his Great Spirit flings volant wings
and travels to ever-expanding edges.

I await the freeing of my spirit.

Day Sixteen

in the *morning sun*, after a cold **night**,
the Spirit resurrects my old bones
from a long evening's death.
I stare at the ^{dawning} orb's *glory,*
shut my eyes and see waves of red—
nothing is more powerful than the *sun*-sea,
flowing in my head, sinews, and veins,
breathing God's Spirit into my spirit.

the sound of the *sun* is heard in the wind—
the miraculous breathing of regeneration.
and then there is Sacred Silence,
as when a caterpillar spins a cocoon
and *transfigures* into a monarch—
the methuselah migrating to Mexican mountains.

at *light's* end, peregrination begins,
carrying memories of swelling oceans,
of long strong seas under ^{rising} *suns,*
and the *awakening* of stars and m()()n.

I see **star dark** heavens, m()()n dancing *light,*
planet Proxima Centauri[b] and Sirius[a].
I am searching for another earth to wake.
I await another sea-swarmed planet—
I know the billion galaxies have more,
as I wade in the sea's shallows in m()()n-light.

Day Seventeen

frozen **blackness**, numb stars, frosty Sirius—
only lonely Venus slightly *shines*
as **night** transforms into day and the *sun pierces* the horizon.
the blood-red sky is God's face painted by the warm orange
^{ascending orb}, casting a golden chatoyant on the ocean
that the *walk-on-water-Jesus* could step on.
the chimerical aisle beckons me to join.

I snorkel to the reef, spear two fish, clean and cook them
for Luke and me, who eat and drink the last of the water I brought—
we will have to depend on the rainwater caught in the boat.

the day is suffocated by **darkness**,
strangling every pulse of *light.*
she lays dead in the arms of mother earth,
sleeping peacefully until the morning *sun* ^{resurrects}

Day Eighteen

full bloody m()()n, *red-streaked* Mars,
bright robust shining Venus
dominate the *pre-dawn* sky—
then Helios *bursts* the horizon,
as seabirds ^{wing} across its face.
the ocean waves cant, billow, bReaK—
the sea *heaves* itself on shore
throwing barrels of white water on the beach
just within the reach of the scurrying sandpipers and seagulls.

the seashore sound is perfect to my ear—
fortissimo, *caesura*, fortissimo, *caesura*
(the alluvial-beat on the sandy littoral).
deep full bass, then high-pitched snare,
crashing cymbals, then *shakers* and *sizzlers.*

Day Nineteen

dark clouds **obscure** the morning horizon;
I can't see the lustrous majestic *sun*
but shafts of *light* break through the gray—
the *parousia* of promise, the *brilliant epiphany.*
I need not wait until an awful end
as I watch the wind ^{uplift} the pelicans
and hear the ocean as the voice of *Glory*—
all I need to know of the divine narrative
is written in waves ^{lifted} by the zephyrs,
to be read as they ^{rise} and spill over.

the *sun* at _{dusk} paints the western horizon
with the colors of murder—
sanguinity dripping into the sky.
every creature becomes breathlessly quiet.
and then the stars start to sing.

Day Twenty

I stare and gaze at the ^{rising} Helios—
a present *parousia* and magnificent apotheosis—
I watch *sunrise* break the gray horizon
casting an aisle wonderfully chimerical and surreal—
on the billowing ocean to the littoral
where I stand, *sun-drenched*, in shallow water
watching the aisle spread wider ^{as the sun ascends higher}
until the sky and sea are ablaze in *brilliance*—
I *run, wade, and dive* into liquid illumination.

then I spot a pod of seven or eight dolphins
lingering around the reef, looking for small fish.
I paddle out among them, and they stay to play around me—
circling me on my surfboard, leaping out of the water
throwing jelly balls into the air with their deft nostrums,
then catching them again—doing this over and over
like dolphin volleyball, dolphin baseball, or dolphin soccer—
little did I know that they would become my friends,
visiting this reef and me on my surfboard again and again—

Luke and I eat a meal of fish I speared at the reef;
we drink rainwater caught in the boat and watch sunset—
later, in the southern **night** sky crescent m()()n, Sirius, and Venus
like three sisters closely cluster—they cheer the **darkness**

Day Twenty-one

as ^{dawn} arrives, the eastern clouds
are painted with streaks of pink, then yellow—
as I watch the ^{sunrise} this morning
through colored clouds *streaked* and o u t s t r e t c h e d
I think of godwits tirelessly winging
thousands of miles, never touching _{down}
and albatross ^{soaring} over pelagic waters months at a time

I watch the bright ^{rising} disk showing itself
and pelicans *sky-surfing* the breakers
gliding, soaring on continuous lefts
on the sea that rolls in from the northeast—

wind *gusts blow me into bird*
winging, soaring, pinions outstretched
volant above the frenzied ocean

the sun _{sinks} sleepily into the western horizon,
sky **darkens**, stars flash, m()()n ^{rises—}
only the white wave rush can be seen and heard—
all else is quiet in the kingdom

Day Twenty-two

in pre-dawn an orange girth circles earth
clouds and sea are barely separated on the horizon
the *sun* appears in a slit between the two
(just long enough to see the *glory*)
then disappears behind the thick gray
leaving an *afterglow* on the azimuth

I know the *sun*—
its certain *slant* and **heavy** light
I know the sea—
its constant *break* and **heavy** fall

the *sun* and sea are miraculous sisters
spun by the same Spirit-Creator—
Luke and I are like brothers, sharing meals of fish,
drinking rainwater collected in the bottom of my skiff

the *sun* slides into the western sea
like a dolphin silently _{submerging}
like a whale _{diving} into the pelagic _{deep}
where **darkness** hides half of eternity

Day Twenty-three

light-waves and ocean-waves *merge and mingle*
casting on the rollers a shimmering aisle
I paddle my board into the *sun-soaked* surf
and catch BrEakeRs running to the right and left

I paddle back out and find myself next to the dolphin pod again
they are ^{emerging}—sucking air through their blow holes (*puuush!*),
then _{submerging} sleekly into the cerulean sea—
they linger around me for a long time, wanting to play—
they hurl the jelly balls with their nostrums
and then quickly swim to catch them again—
they do this for quite a while until the *sun* ghosts away
and they *disappear*, like a group of phantoms, without a sound

under *bright* m()()nlight and sight of the Milky Way
I sit on my board in my own swirling surfing galaxy
waiting for a beauty to come my way—
I stroke furiously to catch a breaker
when, all of a sudden, I'm flung headlong
and fall _{under the lip} of the event horizon
sucked _{down} into the vortex of a **black** whorl—
I swim out on the other side as through a wormhole
and body-surf a smaller roller all the way to shore!

Day Twenty-four

^{sunrise} on soft silver-rolling-surf—
the orange disk slowly ^{ascends,}
turns into **bold**-gold, then mellow-yellow
sliding through the morning clouds
beaming down on broKeN-open ocean—
sun-on-wind-on-waves are my companions
as I paddle into southwestern zephyrs—
an old surfer, still gliding on the rush
as sea crests, crashes, crumbles into mush

as always, my golden retriever, Luke, and I fish—
we catch several blues and spots, cook them and feast

the day dies like we all should—
silently, without protest, and brilliantly,
not expecting any applause, though that may be—
the colors of death are pleasant to the eyes

Day Twenty-five

this morning I ^{rise} to catch brilliant *Helios*
in its *parousia* and magnificent *apotheosis*—
God ^{dawns} in ocean morning presence
in *sunlight* playing in breaking surf,
tumbling froth, surging sallies,
in pelicans' sky-surfing undulations,
seagulls ^{climbing} sun-soaked air,
sea falcons ^{spiriting} azure sky
^{clutching} wriggling seabass in their talons
loggerheads paddling toward sargassum
spinners twisting, jacks ^{leaping}
sandpipers scurrying in *thin* shallows
rays ^{rocketing} from _{deep} to sight
dolphins dallying, porpoising in ocean roll
(the very ones I have come to know)—
the ocean so alive with beautiful souls!

Luke and I eat the fish I caught, drink rainwater,
and lie down for the night as we watch
evening stars appear like angels of the *parousia*
harbingers of the coming *dawn*

Day Twenty-six

I walk the desolate beach with my dog, Luke,
as the *sun* ^{rises} from the h o r i z o n
everywhere is presence—
white water _{falling down} the line
cascading in ocean rhythm and rhyme

wind picks up *light* and throws it all around
sun ^{raises} seabirds' ^{flight}
shedding the **heaviness of night—**

I see the sower of miracles

darkness _{descends} like a hammer blow
nailing the *sun* in a coffin—
she is buried in earth under stars
until the next day's ^{resurrection}

Day Twenty-seven

the sea is spirit, soul of the *sun*
ocean reflects her ^rising^ *glory*
she mirrors her transforming colors—
incarnadine, tangerine, vermillion

the waves are wind-on-water, billowing brine,
I *lean* into the ghosting gusts
and *ride* the morning's zephyrs
as the *sun* ^hangs\ ten^ on the horizon

swimming around the island
my golden retriever chases the day—
nostrils snorting just above the surface
legs kicking ~underneath~ like crazy

he's heading for his wilderness
to chase the dolphins riding the waves—
his is a world of savage scents
wild sounds and **wild** God

when he returns to me
we head into the rolling sea
where we take turns body-surfing to shore
*and all we **wild** want is **wild** more*

the day ends as it begins—
sky spattered red, clouds colored pink
the full circle of life and death—
the *inspiration* of spirit
the *expiration* of breath

Day Twenty-eight

conscious of a nearby presence
then coming into view, I see
m()()n fox dancing in the shadows
prancing in the sand dunes
cautiously sauntering up to me,
not stalking, but approaching as a friend

the fox's gaze *awakens my primordial spirit*
urging me to abandon all and go wild

the fox stays with me for quite awhile
(while my dog, Luke, is off, exploring the island)
until the *sun* plunges into the western azimuth
and the wind swirls from the south—
all around me is the wonder of God—
as light _{falls} from the sky
and the fox wanders off in **darkness**

Day Twenty-nine

m()()n-struck fox runs to the ocean
where I paddle out and catch fire
in ember-orange flames of ^{dawn—}
skimmers, sliding on waves, swish past me
cawing seagulls ^{swirl overhead}
the dolphins I know *appear* like saviors
as *sunlight* bounces off my surfboard—
I am ocean, I am animal
sea-blood flows in my mammalian bones
too **heavy** for me to ^{fly and soar}

Luke and I walk the beach on the Caribbean side,
eat the fish I speared earlier, drink rainwater, then sleep—
comforted and consoled by the ceaseless rolling waves
under an evening of stars flooding the **dark deep** skies

Day Thirty

fox! lightning!
dashing through the sand dunes
darting on the ocean's horizon
quick quintessence revealed awakens spirit
to grab one moment of trillions
as the fox saunters and time slows—
a minute glaciates into eons and eons,
as the fox stops (my heart races)
and stands a few feet ahead—
a magnificent, God-breathing quadruped

the fox melts into the western sky
and disappears like ghosting spirit
I sleep and dream of wilderness
running as long as m()()nlight lasts

in this dream I slide out of my lungs
and slip into primordial ocean
my legs turning into dolphin fins—
so much earth is sea
that sun rises everywhere
and **darkness** is the same as *light*

will I ever run out of life?

Day Thirty-one

I am destined to trace ^{the risings}
peaking in summer ^{zeniths}
as gods transform into clouds
and rollers turn my thoughts into ghosts

undulating ocean in my brain
crests,   heaves
    crashes   hollows—
my heart pumping wave after wave
reaching every beach of my body—
dawn dolphins in my veins
tide ^{rises} and _{falls} in my blood—
in every cell I am ocean

as sea surges in my body and surrounds
I paddle out in zephyr-rollers
    _{under} ^{rising} Venus and crescentM()()n—
then surf a glorious wave of God
and paddle back out among the dolphin pod
admiring their glistening fins in m()()nlight
feeling, for a moment, I could be one of them

I surf to shore with my companion, Luke,
the sweetest soul, who shares the love of life with me,
swimming the ocean together, catching fish, sharing meals—
enjoying the *zen-of-nowness*, feeling the *essential* real

Day Thirty-two

Luke and I walk the ocean as I trace the flight ^{of the sun}
and I ruminate the l o n g path of man's searchings—
how humans first r e a c h e d out for a God-touch
(like the *hand-drawings* in ancient Chauvet caves)
and how humans first believed in ^{resurrection life}
(like the *Egyptian mummies* waiting to ^{rise})

human spirits yearn to feel the Spirit divine:
the Syro-Phoenician woman fingering Jesus' hem,
the meditating monk groping for moksha,
the native agonizing in the *sun* dance
hoping to grasp the Mystery's meaning,
and all the martyrs praying for the palpable Presence
as their flesh is ripped and torn away

Day Thirty-three

full m()()n, drunk with *light,*
woBblEs on the western horizon
as it *pulls* the ocean into a King tide—
Venus and Sirius *lord* the night's sky
until **darkness** is stabbed and s l o w l y dies

roaring *sun*-wind roils the rumpled ocean
zig-zag zephyrs race across the *sun's* face—
the earth is alive with brave beauty
rolling sky and sea into a *scroll* of mystery

I interpret the palimpsest
as I watch wave-step-upon-wave
leaving footprint after footprint of froth
as watery souls appear for a moment
then just as quickly turn into ghosts

I paddle my surfboard into the breaking surf
Luke paddles out with me—I can tell he wants
to mount the surfboard, so I slide off, untie my leash
and help him up—then I shove the board into a small roller
which he rides, sitting sphinx-like, all the way to shore!

Day Thirty-four

bright m()()n and Venus **dominate** the night's sky
until the more glorious one eclipses them
flocks of seabirds *tango* in morning *light*
they dance in ^{dawn}, ^{rising} as one, _{descending} as one
swoooooping, undulating, *spiraling*, ^{cresting},
looking like *ocean waves* in the sky,
they soar ^{above} the ocean wilderness
whipped with flashing wind-swept spindrifts

newborn loggerheads *scurry* to the surf
a hammerhead d r i f t i n g in the shallows
searches for a quick morning meal
my dog, Luke, chases it with u n l e a s h e d zeal
as pelicans sky-surf the breakers

everylivingthing is beautifully bold—
the bright ocean, the silk sky, the fecund earth
in the solitude of silence and *lightness* of being—
even sunset is as beautiful as God

Day Thirty-five

the lure of the ocean catches me, seizes me—
I am enraptured by its waves, peaks, and crests.
I want to immerse my body, soul, and spirit
into its force, liquid flesh, and brilliant rush—
so I run and dive into the sea headfirst.
my dog, Luke, follows—darting, dashing, plunging
into the shallows, then paddling like crazy,
keeping his head above the turbulent waters.
he won't go under, as I do, being able to hold my breath.
I go back to shore, grab my long surfboard,
paddle out, catch a long right that takes me into paradise—
as I surf a moment-of-God, an instant of divinity
unfolded and revealed for a few seconds of eternity—
I overcome my pain (for now) by surfing the ocean!

Luke and I are running very low on rain water—
I pray to the Creator God to bring us a storm

Day Thirty-six

I wake to the throbbing ache in my pancreas
as rolling *sunbeams* undulate like ocean
I gather in warmth as if pulling in a seine
(I envision long ago the native fishermen
chanting, tugging, pulling, catching—
the women coming down from the village
with empty platters on their heads)
it's the mystery of *daybreak*
the gift of the Spirit lavishing the coast

everything sacred is round
like the platters on their heads:
the curve of the horizon
the bright golden *orb*
the planets circling the *sun*
the trillion swirling galaxies
the palm frond canopies
the tubular waves just now rolling in
the spirit-wheels of the cherubim
the great hoop of life—
the ^{sunrise} and _{sunset} winds

Luke and I fish, catch a few,
which I cook—and we eat—
we drink the last of our rain water
before going to sleep under the stars
lulled by the ceaseless sound of waves

Day Thirty-seven

a ball of *brilliant brightness,*
the savage *sun* ^{ascends} the sky.
held open by offshore zephyrs,
as beastly breakers bite the beach.
I am devoured by *sun* and sea
eaten to my quick by raw divinity—
brute nature, beautifully brave,
oozes with miraculous mana—
the divine is seen in ocean wind,
revealed in the acropetal waves
that rise, curl, heave, and pearl—
the awesome alchemy of the sea

an orange rind ensconces the western horizon
the pulp is juicy *pulsating* ocean—
I watch pelicans **penetrate** the azimuth
becoming **d a r k** g h o s t s o f g o n e
melting into the sun _{just now falling} ‾
somewhere near is f o r e v e r . . .
I see it in the swirling advection
I hear it in anapestic waves
and allophonic bReaKers

Day Thirty-eight

the *light* s t r e t c h e s   a l o n g   t h e   h o r i z o n
like a strand of orange yarn
pulled out straight by a kitten

then the *light* is gathered into one tight ball
of bright crimson turning gloriously yellow—
the *colors* of God just before dawn

I watch swirling sea-falcons _{dive} into the waters
stretching their necks, extending their talons—
they skim the blue shallows and scoop up fish

I listen to the ocean, an oracle of beauty,
speaking to my thalassic spirit and marine soul
I hear everlasting *glory* in unending waves

then Helios *races* swiftly to its ultimate zenith
like an Indian galloping bareback to the west
chasing the Great Mystery of life and death . . . . .

Luke and I are very thirsty—two days without water—
I pray to the Creator God for a heaven-sent storm

Day Thirty-nine

ocean sound, tubular round,
spirals through my open eardrums
ocean wind, *ghost thin,*
penetrates my earthly membranes—
I am awash in sea and *sun*
having nowhere to go but here-and-now

I swim out to the reef with my spear gun
and shoot three angel fish (feeling guilty—
but Luke and I have to eat to live)
I cook their pink flesh and we feast,
lasting out the day with walks on the beach

_{setting sun,} magnificently coloring
the cloudy western horizon,
_{descends} into my innermost being
as our day is drained into **darkness**—
I feel nothing but the here-and-now
and am incredibly thirsty

Day Forty

in **dark benthic depths** *dawn* was dead
until a crimson bloody orb ^{arose}—
the miracle of earth o p e n i n g like a hand

I watch morning hues runIntoEachother

the *sun* fingers the thin horizon
painting the cumulous with luscious sheen
crushing the morning cold with her palms

I ooze a colorful psalm

the sky is *falling* into ocean
wave upon wave soaks my pain
I have gotten used to suffering—
I don't always see the sun

but **darkness** cannot ruin me
as I tightly grip promises
of seeing the dolphins ^{rise} from the deep
and swim with me near the reef

this evening I see a sea-hawk swoop down
on the ocean catching a fish in its talons—
how I admire its grace, dexterity, and power!

Day Forty-one

during the night it rained (thank Almighty Creator!)
I awake, as does Luke, and we drink and drink—
lapping up water from the boat's bottom with our tongues

soft gray *spreads* like butter across the sky
light-gray, like seagulls' wings, *slides* across the waves
the orange *orb* appears long enough to believe
then disappears behind smooth silver clouds—

mankind has waited millennia to witness the Parousia

unexpectedly *waves* of heat
r o l l   i n t o t h e   b r e a k i n g o c e a n
(like Amazon blowing into the Yukon)
for an epiphanic moment I envision
aquatic *zoa* flowing around the heavenly throne—
sea-falcons, sea-otters, sea-horses, and dolphins
I just now see ᵉᵃᵖⁱⁿᵍ *out of the ocean*

the *sun* zeniths, arcs westward
silently ₑₑₛcₑₙₑₛ into a blend of roseate colors
as the dying *sun* paints ᵗʰᵉ ˢᵏʸ with blood

Day Forty-two

sun! fire!
red *flames* reflecting in the shallows
orange glow flushing the sky
bright halo radiating the horizon—
I scan its imminent azimuth
as it ^{rises} toward its ^{zenith}

o *sun*, you were worshiped in your ^{heights}—
virgins spilled their blood for you
worshipful natives *pierced* their flesh
you were **darkened** when he was crucified
you were breaking sorrow
when he was rising back to life

Day Forty-three

the ocean is bright open! brilliant
in the bold blazing ^{sunrise} on the sea
I, as a sun-dancer, seek Wakan Tanka,
I see my name written in a vision: "sky-seahawk-fox"
revealer of light, dancer in liberating *sun-flight,*
^{glider} on bird's wings, ^{flying} into realms of far ocean,
prancer in m()()n-light, vulpine, retiary, spirited.

in my vision quest, I view my Spirit-God afresh—
he mingles with my spirit, he inspires my soul,
he lives in me, and I in him, a branch of the sacred tree—
I cannot lose him, and he can't give up on me—

I surf during _{sunset} painted pink and red
until the day expires in splattered blood—
I sleep the entire night dreaming of my God,
as it rains slightly—a gift from the Creator

Day Forty-four

Spirit God, be with me in my vision quest
blow the holy wind through me
breathe the Holy Spirit into me
I want to see the spirits beyond my sight
before my spirit ^{ascends} into the afterlife—
come! Lord Spirit! pneumatic Creator!
let me see now what I will see later—
appear! reveal! enlighten! infuse!
speak to me, Spirit God, open the veil
between the here-and-now and what is to come
show me the apotheosis of the *Parousia*
open the door of apocalyptic paradise—
let me smell heaven's flowers before they bloom!
let me see the light behind the celestial doors!

piercing my chest with large fish-hooks
leaning away from the palm where I tied the fishing lines
I enact my own version of the *sun* dance
seeking through pain, greater than my cancer,
to see my Creator and drink his grace—
(blood, blood—blood of his love
runs down my breasts like tears)
I'm in a swoon of *sun*-stroke
as Mystery and Majesty bow my head
and excruciating Power strips my flesh.
I am naked before God, bent before my Lord—
I see his face *shining* in strength
more *brilliant* than the *sun* beating my back.
I fall to my knees and the hooks gouge deeper
I call to the Great Spirit, who is my Creator!

I am transported in spirit to the heavenly adytum
and see the One who is, who was, who is to come,
the Beginning and the End, the First and the Last,
the Alpha and Omega, eternal God-man, the Amen,
who is standing next to a sea of glassy waves
with myriad dolphins porpoising and pelicans gliding

with a multitude of *zoa* gamboling in a field before him—
celestial *zoa* with multiple wings, full of eyes within,
having many faces and myriad divine shapes,
who are created for God's pleasure and delight
and then replicated on earth in fleshly form—
born to mirror the heavenly Beings with variegated
feet, hands, paws, faces, fins, feathers, and wings:
swinging monkeys, gliding falcons, leaping frogs,
jumping kangaroos, grazing cows, galloping horses,
winging cormorants, hopping rabbits, slithering snakes,
crawling lizards, climbing ibex, porpoising dolphins,
swimming sea-serpents, breeching whales, drifting seahorses,
swirling kestrels, diving pelicans, roaring lions,
paddling sea-turtles, crouching tigers, loping okapis,
stinging scorpions, scavenging vultures, chest-beating gorillas,
stampeding wildebeests, waddling ducks, migrating monarchs,
wandering godwits, nectar-sipping hummingbirds, eye-staring alligators—
crowing roosters, cackling crows, cooing morning-doves,
laughing hyenas, rocketing stingrays, creeping lizards,
stalking felines, retrieving canines, howling wolves,
salmon-fishing grizzlies, seabass-snatching ospreys, lumbering elephants,
desert-trekking camels, forest-dwelling foxes, speedy roadrunners—
all as old as leviathans, and young as newborn behemoths

then a voice roars, as loud as crashing giant waves, telling me,
"write what you see and hear and send it to your descendants:
the Creator who is, who was, and who is to come
has seen the violence humanity has done on earth,
murdering each other and killing creatures for greed:
let all the mounted animal-trophies breathe!
let them jump off the walls to earth and sea!
let museum specimens come back to life!
let etherized, impaled insects escape glass cases—
swallowtails, monarchs, hawk moths, dragonflies!
let monarchs migrate to Mexico again!
let all sharks regain their fins!
let all elephants regrow their tusks!
let all buffaloes graze the plains!
let seahorses drift in the oceans!

let rhinoceros resurrect their horns!
let carrier pigeons fly the skies again!
let wild saber-tooth tigers unfreeze!
and let wooly mammoths and native American horses
be free to breathe, breed, and run!
let the caged circus lions be freed!
as well as the chained tigers and elephants!
let the zoos' fences and doors fly open!
let all animals and humans live in harmony!
let the feral cats find welcoming homes!
let the wild dogs find friendly companions!"

then I hear every tongue utter his praises—
the lips of marine and aerial creatures call his Name,
all subterranean, terrestrial, and celestial beings sing Hallelujah—
joined by trillions of cherubim and seraphim—
all the universe with all its collective breath
chanting glory to the One who is, who was, and who is to come,
the Alpha and Omega, the Beginning and the End!

I am transported back to the seaside
where I see waves and waves on end—
forming, rolling, cresting, breaking
blue hyaline turning into white foam—
realizing that earth, as much as heaven, is my home!

Day Forty-five

slowly stars vanish, half m()()n rocks in the west
the *solar* artist (before she herself appears)
paints the eastern horizon—
crimsonStreaks roseateSwaths redSwipes
the *sun* rolls IntoSkyIntoSeaIntoSpirit

I feel like the pierced sun-dancer
bleeding into the Creator
as _{sundown} ends gloriously red—
everylivingthing is silent
except the stars singing God

Day Forty-six

not in the blink of an eye
the *parousia* is a s l o w epiphany
transforming blackness into ghost-gray
then coloring clouds ^{hanging on the horizon}__
sanguine, roseate, and salmon

m()()nlight dwindles, planets fade
until I no longer see Venus—like Jesus
who became spirit and can ghost into wind
or blend with the gathering of seagulls
on shore just now waiting for ^{dawn to spring}

I, too, have an eye on the east
when *(all of a sudden!)* I spot the fox
I know, scampering down the seacoast
coming to rest on a nearby sand dune
where together we catch a warm revelation

later, **darkness,** _{deep} as water, settles on the surf
crescent m()()n, cradle-shaped, rocks in the s l o w ^{sky}
Venus *sparkles* in all her lonely glory
Sirius and other stars *appear* one by one
until the **darkness** is no longer alone

Day Forty-seven

the clouds and seas are like white stallions
running in southern zephyrs under *breaking sun*—
manes *flying*, billows *galloping*, waves *spin-drifting*

all morning the skies and breakers rush north
(the Spirit dancing, the Spirit flowing)
God revealing himself in *sun*, sea, and wind

not one flowing-living-gliding-winding-thing
dies even at _{sundown}—the night ^{jumps} alive
with surprise in the **dark** as _{deep} as God

Luke and I are terribly thirsty, for three days having not drunk—
licking the boat's bottom for whatever liquid we can suck—
I find a coconut, cut it open, and share the nectar with Luke
(not much, but enough to barely sustain)

Day Forty-eight

without warning—
hurricane ocean,
scourged by wind
whipping waves
into frenzy and froth—
wild white water,
hurls, spills, crashes
whitecaps as far as sight
roaring sea-beasts
turgid, turbulent,
rushing, raging
spewing spindrifts
breakers tumbling
as the cyclone twists,
turns, swirls, breaks
pummeling the coast—
as the brute beast
bends nature
bullies seas
into heave, growl,
ghoul—not discriminating
whose marrow it sucks—
shores, homes, trees,
thinner structures—man
as it dumps
heaps of water
deeper than despair
that there's no God
of Noah near

through all of this
I hide on shore
under my lean-two
attached to my boat
with Luke, my retriever—
while wind, sand, foam
throw fury in our faces—

at least, we are grateful
for the water-downfall!

Day Forty-nine

a **wave-stampede** *RushesTheShore*
as far as I can see, the ocean gallops
from naked benthic rolling depths
to my bare feet in the shallows—
I'm walking in the wild,
stepping in the hallowed

ocean animaling under elephant sky
lunges, lurches, zoos to shore like Serengeti zebras
nostrils flared, legs kicking, manes flailing *in the wind*

I used to paddle out among these huge beasts
and surf them for all their surprise
but now that I am weaker, I ride the big ones with my eyes!

in the evening I walk the ocean with my dog
following our silhouettes in m()()n shadow
admiring a glowing aisle cast by Venus
gazing at s t a r s   s t r e w n in the heavens
thinking of the multitude of natives
who, centuries ago, scanned this same horizon
never imagining that wave after white wave
would rush and quash their home

Day Fifty

sound of the sea entrances me
^{transcends}, transports, ^{raptures},
wings me to exotic shores
where I envision native fishermen
in glowing dawn, *dragging* boats
in the sand into plummeting surf
hauling dragnets, hoping for fish,
grabbing Spirit from the ribbon-sky
chanting _{under} ^{hovering caws}
backs glistening, fish ^{leaping},
pulling in the ocean sun

the sun sets in glorious death colors—
ruby red, crimson, scarlet, vermillion—
like red wine splashed all over the horizon.
I am drunk on the Divine, inebriated in Spirit,
stumbling into sleep, falling into dreams—
where beach goes on forever and waves never stop—
I am lost in water, I am swallowed up in God

Day Fifty-one

morning deluge drowns solar sky
immersing shore and sea in phantoms of gray
rain, fiercely sacred, is *zoapoien*
rebirthing earth—fecund, green, pristine—
palingenesis—getting the face of God again!

flipper tracks in wet sand tell the story
of journey's end from the Sargasso Sea
and return to her nativity—
in the autumn evening of their births
the newborn scurry into the rushing tide
hearing, for the first time, God!

I imbibe **night** sky, inhale stars,
breathe sea into my being—
I am neither young or old
I am a wave rollingCrestingCrashing,
surging, sallying, *ghosting* into God's breath

Day Fifty-two

I ache in my back—stabbing pain and dreadful dolor
I wear my back-brace all day long, not just when I surf
I hardly sleep, even though the sand is soft under my blanket—
every day I hope to see the fox again—he awakes my primordial spirit
and every day I hope to see the dolphins emerging from the sea—
they are all signs that life is precious, life is rare

as I walk the ocean and listen to the rhythmic waves
I speak to some souls who've gone before me—
noteworthy scholars, dear friends, and personal relations
(even one who fought in the American revolution)—
I pray they are resting in the risen Spirit of Jesus.
I chant, *"Iesous, Pneuma Theos (Jesus—Spirit God),*
be their Kurios, Soter Christos (Lord—Savior Christ)"

as I stroll, I watch my golden retriever, Luke,
romping, darting, dashing, and galloping in the shallows—
free as wind, liberated in spirit, pursuing seabirds,
racing breaking waves, running into the white water—
he is so alive, he makes me both laugh and cry,
as we scamper together in the *sea-sun*, chasing ghosts!

in the evening we eat the fish I speared
and drink the rainwater our boat caught

Day Fifty-three

the sea is very alive today—jumping, thumping,
throwing its surf onto reef and shore—I want more!
(enough *to free* my spirit with the living quick!)
I join the wave in its quintessence—I power into the break,
thrust under, duck-dive, submerge, emerge, paddle deeper—
wait for the set to form, pull like crazy, jump to my feet,
bend my knees, get balanced, thrill at being in the waves' wall,
pushing me all the way to shore in crazy white water

Day Fifty-four

o Soter Theos (oh, Savior God)
cleanse me in the immaculate ocean—
o Pneuma Iesous (oh, Spirit Jesus)
wash me in the purifying wind—
I have come to the seashore to be rinsed in the divine,
to be scrubbed in the celestial sky and emerald ocean.

I am seeking Spirit-God in *sea-sun-wind,*
I am making the invisible visible in my poems,
as the Spirit-Creator becomes the created word.
I scan seabirds soaring and flying high above me
(seagulls, pelicans, cormorants, ospreys)
headed for better fishing in thalassic cays!

Day Fifty-five

a violent *anemos*—a windstorm—assaults the sea,
marauding white-capped breakers storm the shore!
all around is strong wind, stronger sea and *pneuma*—
I feel *Iesous Pneuma Theos (Jesus Spirit-God)*.
I see his visage in the waves just now taking shape
and breaking into open faces with lips and curls—
how awesome the sight of divine billows rolling,
flowing down the line in rhythm and rhyme
as the once-violent ocean forms rows of glorious surf—
I paddle out with Luke and we catch some beauties.

Day Fifty-six

as **Cimmerian** clouds blow across the eastern horizon,
the **aphotic, caliginous** skies explode with rain—
Luke and I wait out the storm under the lean-two,
as violent rain-gusts pound the sea and shore—
I am overwhelmed by the furious force of nature—
this goddess can be as tempestuous as she is amiable;
though I don't worship her, I completely revere her
because she has power to unleash celestial torrents!
I believe in God *and* the spirit-gods of the universe—
they move the sun—moon—stars—wind—waves
(as heaven touches earth and handles **caliginous clay**)—
the elemental spirits govern, the potent *archai* rule,
the spiritual authorities reign, the invisible powers control—
Jesus, monophysite God-man, the Premier and Primogenitor,
rules over all, like the sunlight now covering the shore!

Day Fifty-seven

rainstorm, ocean squall, thunderous skies and seas—
waves breaking loud as jets taking off into the atmosphere—
as big God unfetters torrential gales on the coastline,
and a tropical cyclone heaves **dark** heavens on shore—
Luke and I huddle under the lean-two tied to our boat
until a gust blows it away and I have to chase it down the beach.
I bring it back and tie it to the boat, stake it, then wait out the storm
with Luke by my side, shivering, shuddering, and shaking.
I pray to Jesus, Spirit-God, the almighty seven-fold Spirit:
Iesous, Pneuma-Theos (Jesus, Spirit-God)
Didaskalos, Rabboni, Huios Anthropou (Teacher, Rabbi, Son of Man)
Thaumasiotatos, Therapon, Iatros (Thaumaturgist, Therapist/Healer, Physician)
Kurios, Christos, Parakletos (Lord, Christ, Paraclete)
Logos, Eikon Theou, Prototokos (Logos, Image of God, Premier)
Ktistes, Apaugasma, Charakter (Creator, Radiant One, Express Image)
Pantokrator Huios, Soter (Almighty Son, Deliverer)
please be with us through this potent devastating storm—
keep us from dying before our time has come!

Day Fifty-eight

God is Spirit. God is wind. The ocean is *pneuma, aeros, anemos, zoe*—
all mingling with each other, flowing, breathing, rolling, rushing.
I am the most alive when I am in God's *pneuma* of life and light—
sunshine penetrating the ocean-rollers, wind blowing on the water—
breathing *zoe* into all creation, shining light on every sentient being.
Praise the Divine! I exult in the vital verve of nature! I enjoy God!

Luke and I swim out to the reef to fish, have some luck
then we return to our boat where I clean them and cook—
washing them down with the plenteous rainwater we've collected

Day Fifty-nine

m()()n island bobbing in the watery sky
overlooks my isle ^{floating} in the ocean
bright *winds* stir the sea of my soul
sea-sky wraps around my circular horizon

the eastern *orb* ^{surfaces}, gushing luminaires—
I am immersed in liquid *light,*
as I watch the Invisible move the Atlantic
hear sun-dawn spirit fly by quick
like monarchs thin as *wind—*
each one, real as God, a sign!

I decipher the message of parchment sky—
the vellum *sun*, the palimpsest m()()n.
the divine *semeia* I must decode
are *brilliant* dawn, *radiant* zenith, mellow dusk
until my mind crumbles like old papyrus touched

I catch a glimpse of the fox scampering down the beach
I watch the sun fall and the m()()n rise into the heavens
casting an aisle on the ocean—an aisle I could walk on

Day Sixty

I'm seeking *sila*—the air spirit and spiritual power
that permeates the universe, nature, sky, and wind.
I'm finding *puha*—that deep dynamo that flows
throughout the world and sustains its balance.
I'm inscribing prayer-stones with divine messages
from the *sun*, the m()()n, and the constellations.

in the ancient spirit I've been here thousands of years—
I've seen droughts, storms, *sun torrents*, and many m()()ns—
I've seen the *sun* break, the m()()n bleed, and sky turn **opaque.**
what I've witnessed I've inscribed on ostraca and stones
to be read by generations who stroll this ocean
and discover that the *mana* of *sila and puha* is God's poem.

Day Sixty-one

the day w a n d e r s like bedouins roaming the Negev
the sea meanders, *bends, turns, twists,* ^{rises}, _{crashes,}
crumbles into millions of particles of foaming *lights*

long after I'm dead and quickly gone to ghost
this galaxy will implode into a massive **black** hole.
if I were not spirit, I would tumble into it

but I will be in the new heaven and new earth
somewhere beyond the *sun*, m()()n, and *stars,*
where wraiths congregate and spirits gather.

Day Sixty-two

I'm wonderstruck by peach pink ^{sun-up} turning crimson
like the millions of red crabs marching to the ocean—
the entire sky and coast is painted in vermilion.
hundreds of pelicans ^{soar overhead}, headed to northern seas
where there are fish galore—more than can be imagined.
I walk the beach with Luke and admire the swelling surf—
we can't resist—I enter with my surfboard, Luke paddling alongside—
when we reach the reef, Luke wants to get on the board,
so I push him into a moderate break which he rides to the beach.
I holler after him, "Ride it all the way to shore!"
He is the magic surf-rider, the superior canine long-boarder!

Day Sixty-three

I turn my back to the sea like most of the *moia* on Easter Island
and stare at the western skies becoming **dark and gloomy.**
then I turn to see **thunderbolts** *striking* the morning ocean—
calm waves quickly turning *wild* as the wind *hurls* them

I tour the island Atlantic-side and Caribbean-side, looking for God—
he is here!—in the rain, in the ocean, in the wind, in the palms
swaying, glistening bright green—*alive* with the Spirit of Jesus,
moving through all animated souls and beings breathed into life
by the God of creation, the Lord and giver of all things bright!

I walk the beach with my dog, Luke, and spot the dolphins we know—
we swim out to them and join them in play—the highlight of my day!

I hope the *Parousia* won't come as suddenly as Vesuvius
struck the cities Herculaneum and Pompeii,
but Jesus said his *Parousia* would be like lightning
flashing in the clouds from the east to the west
more *brilliant* than the *sun* just now *breaking* through the storm—
suddenly a rainbow arcs majestically on the western horizon
and I am promised that earth will not be flooded by heaven.

Day Sixty-four

slow rollers on the serene green sea
entice me, like sirens, to paddle out and surf.
I want to join the mystic spirits calling me—
to immerse myself in water, wind, and *sun*,
to saturate my spirit with the waters of the ocean—
to drink God, breathe mana, inhale Lord-Spirit,
to be in the divine, to feel verve, to be a part of it—
moving in motion with the *Pleroma*—deity's fullness—
as all this happens in the riding of the swelling wave,
where wind pushes liquid ^{up the face}, and water becomes glacis—
in the ultimate rush of spirited sea, the flowing thaumaturgist!

as I wait for another set of waves to form
I am struck in my left leg!—
pain shooting immediately to my brain!—
a fish biting my calf, then swimming away.
I immediately paddle in, with Luke by my side,
soak up some blood, make a tourniquet—
crying and crying as I try to stop the flood!
(my heart is pounding out of my chest!)
then I cut some fishing line, attach a needle,
and stitch up the wound, screaming to God!
I apply antibacterial cream from the first aid kit,
and drink as much water as I can get down my throat.
for the rest of the day, I cannot do anything
but try to cope with the stabbing pain!

I rehearse the attack in my mind
and come to the only conclusion
that I was bit by a barracuda or a small reef shark
who punctured my flesh, then swam away.

Day Sixty-five

as vertical rays ^{rise} through the coffin
of the long flat atrabilious horizon
gray rain gives way to *apocalyptic* sky
and *sun-strands* break through **heavy clouds**

God is o p e n, the Spirit is **loud**

I hear the mystery of *sun-struck* sea
as morning winds play the waves percussively
which ^{rise} in pitch, blown through tubes,
heave/hollow/round/rip/curl/break/crash

I can't get up, crippled by my pain

the *sun* ruptures **dark** cumulous
as it ^{ascends} toward its ^{zenith}
distancing itself from the ocean
galloping westward to more revelations

the sky unscrolls—I read what's written

despite my pain, I have no other choice but to try to fish—
Luke and I must eat—so I fix a line and cast it in—
luckily I catch a wrasse, which I manage to clean
and cook, so that Luke and I can eat before we sleep

the sky becomes dark—I can't read the sky

as I lay on my blanket my thoughts turn to my sons,
who are my soul, my spirit awakening,
I read their faces like I decipher the sea and *sun*—
they are the only ones I would live and die for

I await the morning—when faith turns to sight

my sons are broken, humbled, expressing meek spirit,
tried by fire, worn by water, always seeking better—

I will go to my grave with their names on my lips.
I will never let anything divide us or eclipse.

Day Sixty-six

my golden retriever, Luke, and I (in pain) wander oceanside
        watching the pelagic waves become thalassic:

windThrust windBend wingTurn sunRend skyChange
        wavePush. peek. glacis. surge and suck. splash and swoosh.

ebb tide. fetch and flash. ^{rise} and $_{fall}$. ^{crest} and $_{crash}$.
        wave bReak. sea splash. pound ground. kick. flush. push

against my flesh. rush gush tide flow shallowingDeep
        clearingAir breakingBack *whiteBurst* in surge

froth $_{down\ tow.}$ the sea. the sea. lines of it.
tons of it. water creator dumping thumping

crashing crushing. l o n g sea. o p e n ocean. holding earth
        through dawn and dusk. long sovereign. lone Lord

untamed. uncut. untrammeled. undivided. moves me.
        move me. make me oceanic. make me sea.

Luke and I drink the rainwater collected in the boat,
        then eat the fish I speared at the reef.

Day Sixty-seven

the morning *sun* breaks the circular horizon
      and moves the ocean to begin its flow and surge.

waves wend me. send me places I haven't stepped. I haven't
      thought. oh, when the wave breaks, its beauty o p e n s

like divinity undressed. God is *unveiled* as Spirit *expressed.*
      light is pushed out of **darkness** and moves euphotic.

everywhere under over in and around, *light* breaks as waves
      snap and hurl their splendid *luminaires* into froth flame.

I ^{rise}. ride. flare. glide. flow fantastic. an *epiphanic*
      flash of soul. of ghost gone incarnate. immaculate. *evanescent.*

untamed. unknown. unchartered. unfettered. unboxed.
      not coaxed. not moved into a zoo. not nailed upon a wall.

not at all stopped. tamed. trammeled. flushed. the gush gladdens
      hope. the roar rages against all sundowns. dive. swim. crash. roll.

Day Sixty-eight

I watch an eyelid *crack the dawn.* the sultry shroud ^{lifts}
      and the single eye *unveils* sky, *beams* seas
as the *lit* disk ember-orange *surges hot* from burning styx,

exorcises **murkiness**, swallows **shadows** between waves,
      makes cool waters ^{rise} and spirit from earth.
it is a day for wind taking *light* and throwing it

all around between the shades and troughs. for drawing
      the long thin horizon line, as circular as the eye
who makes it. it is a day for *epiphany* of color, for the *parousia*

of the *sun's* soft skull rupturing the oval horizon
      flushing it bloodshed red, raw and strange
more crimson than color (hyacinth's firstborn blazing bloom)

wiping **blackness** out of night. stripping sea
      of its mythic mystery. slaying leviathan of its lair and lore
until evening comes rare with spirit-winds

I fall asleep and dream of the heavens and earth
      in the beginning—when earth was formless and empty
and all the world was covered by a **dark, abysmal** sea.

lull and lunge. lunge and lull. water $_{\text{falling}}$ upon water.
      no shore to take the fall. liquid cymbal dropped
on liquid cymbal in the **dark** sound of it all. rush and roll.

roll and rush. but not on shoals, sandbars, reefs.
      deep from caverns the waves $^{\text{leap lunge}}$ $_{\text{plunge}}$ spill.
falling from **dark** pitch crash. crush. roar. *sizzle.*

requiem's breaking dirge. the surge. the slosh.
      the rush crush crash between each fetch and flush
in long stretches of nothing but **darkness** pushing water

into **blacker** spaces. faceless. mirrorless. unconscious
  water making itself seas. waking itself to its own existence
in list. yaw. in *plunge to deep in depths* of gone

going ₍deeper₎. a strangle of water suffocating earth, a liquid ring
  as round as nimbus m()()n—but no *glow*, only **gloom**
in the dirge of surge upon surge flapping fishless fetches

lonely stretches of horizonless seas seizing seas.
  a tumble of **black** rolling into **black** and back again into nothing
but wash wave lunge surge lull crash flush churn.

this sea a monster heaving. heeling in heavy wetness
  in **dark** so fat nothing could wriggle between the cracks
lay leviathan, lay crocodile on all paws, fanning its serpentine

tail over what should be fecund delta, *illumined* soil.
  AllwasWater without *light* AllwasDeep without life, a desert of sea
everywhereGoingnowhere, for there was no horizon

no separation of sea from sight. no beach. no wind of *light*
  to open/break bleak bands/cut/slash/fish darkness out
until the Spirit spoke and smashed damp **black** in half.

Day Sixty-nine

^{climbing} in recurring blooms up gladiola's stem
      popping one after one in cloned effulgence
till *bending* the branch with glory's weight—

the topmost lobe, like the *sun*, begins to make its arch
      above the beloved blue ocean, brother to the silent sky
mother-mouth of every birth and every thirst

I observe the mounting, cresting, pearling, flip, flap, _{fall}, roar.
      the liquid rush, swoosh, sizzle—instant art
splashed, splurged, fanned out, crested, scalloped.

an ocean tongue lapping earth—the shore is ocean lips,
      the waves its mouth—lulling, moaning, spewing foam
from _{fall} fetch pitch crash crush comes

seagull's call and cry. mackerel's flash, the dolphins' push and play
      in salt-sprayed *sunlight*. m()()lit turtles stroking beaches.
water-serpents slithering. angelfish dancing. whales moaning.

greenBrown in swarms of waves one after another breaking
      in blue-froth into so many greens, hundreds of them
more than the forest trees and plants, a roving jungle

of verdant greens holding *sunrays*. lit greens in translucent
      beams, spring-greens popping with visible fish, summercool
bluegreens, layered greens in euphotic dusk shadows

Luke and I walk the ocean shore at sunset, watching our shadows
      grow longer and longer in the evening suncast,
drinking rainwater from the boat, eating our fresh-caught fish.

Day Seventy

a northeastern blows in—I walk facing the wind
knowing that turning around would be heaven—
but in the meanwhile I push against the Boreas gale
bending and bracing against the blustery *force*
knowing that God's Spirit rushes in from the North

I love the Spirit-squall, the gusts of God-storm,
the wind-swept shore, the wind-blown beach.
I watch the seabirds—seagulls, skimmers, pelicans—
soar with the STIFF sea-breeze, riding the turbulent air,
and still I'm walking against the sand-blowing wind

then I turn to where the gale and mistral are at my back
shoving me from behind, thrusting me forward, pushing me faster—
I feel I could take off, *fly* in the *wind*, aviate, and *escape*
the earth's pull on my flesh, the heaviness of being human—
if even for a moment, feeling one with awesome Spirit

the sun drops silently behind the Hesperian horizon *splashing* the sky
with multicolored tinctures and chatoyant hues painted on the clouds—
the chroma of death saturating and spreading out on the far-western plane
(how exquisite and stunning is extinction! how beautiful the last expiration!)
as the sky breathed new light at dawn, so the falling firmament gasps at dusk—
and the spirit it *breathes out* colors the occident gorgeous sanguine.

Day Seventy-one

I walk the ocean, ambling down the beach, chanting:
Iesous, Pneuma-Theos (Jesus, Spirit-God)
Didaskalos, Rabonni, Huios Anthropou (Teacher, Rabbi, Son of Man)
Nazaraios, Tekton, Huios Dauid (Nazarene, Carpenter/Builder, Son of David)
Thaumasiotatos, Therapon, Iatros (Thaumaturgist, Therapist/Healer, Physician)
Huios Theou, Christos, Parakletos (Son of God, Christ, Paraclete)
Despotes, Kerux, Logos (Master, Herald, Logos)
Pleroma, Eikon Theou, Prototokos (Fullness, Image of God, Premier)
Ktistes, Apaugasma, Charakter (Creator, Radiant One, Express Image)
Pantokrator Soter Kurios (Almighty Savior Lord).
Monogenes, Alpha kai Omega, (Unique One, Alpha and Omega)
Arche kai Telos, Emmanouel (Beginning and End, Immanuel)
the waves keep pounding the coastline, soaking the beach,
heaving white water on my feet, beckoning me to dive in,
swim, and surf the glistening breakers surging to the shore.
Luke and I paddle out, as volant pelicans soar overhead—
they are the better surfers, gliding single-file on the crests—
catching wafts of air ᵘᵖᵈʳᵃᶠᵗⁱⁿᵍ from the beachcombers.
how I'd love to be a seabird *flying free and easy—*
sailing like a kite over the ocean, gliding over the sea,
(I'd love to learn kite-surfing, but it's too late now)—
I ride the waves as I always have—paddling, duck-diving,
catching, standing, balancing, sliding, gliding on the wave's face—
moving with the Creator-alive-now-in-creation-surging-splashing—
like a hummingbird levitating for a few moments, sucking nectar,
like a dolphin taking off into the air, spinning, then plashing,
like a golden retriever running in the littoral, chasing seabirds,
like the-walk-on-water-Jesus—as Spirit—as brilliant specter.

Day Seventy-two

the sun rises and is enthroned in the morning clouds—
all day I watch it journey into its zenith and glory

the waves rise into glorious rolling, cresting surf –
Luke and I take turns riding waves into shore

as day transforms into **night** I dream of Christ
but I can hardly speak what I have seen:

Jesus speaks. the Spirit says. living creatures
whirl around the throne, moan, praise, $_{kneel,}$ ^{rise,}

eye the celestial Son of God still feeding
manna to mouths, *light* to **darkness**, liquid words

dripping God. in and out. but I can't articulate.
it is all like. all like. a simile. a metaphor. a poem

spun like heaven from one end of everlasting
to the other. and no one this side of vision can say.

I break through skies but can't push the image out.
I $_{collapse}$ into *sprawl, scrawl, limp, lanky* lines

on leaves, ostraca, papyrus, skins, bones, and paper.
anything thin. but the vision is too big. too *animal*

to capture. too fluid. too spirit to set between
the edges of paper. to spell. to lay flat and dead.

the print cannot rise. the voice lifts. the Spirit.
the flute. the throated longings. breath blown

into a reed. somewhere in there the vision voices.
somewhere in there the poet sees what can't be said.

the restless have to speak. the rested don't.
while the rest await the word. they wait the Lord. the long

strong dreams keep all else asleep. when I wake
I know I've seen but cannot say. apocalypse

comes in waves. and goes. and is. and was.
and is to come what is and was. an everlasting

sound from heaven. an ocean on another shore.
I was there and heard it, I say. I hear

the waves pounding my coast. beating the beach.
the heave, flop, crash. the swoosh, slosh, sizzle.

no human knows, I know. the words can't overflow
the parchment. caught as I am between the waves.

Day Seventy-three

a southern balm washes its way into my air
a solstice swash wiping out cold wind
calling back monarchs, memories, and waves
recapturing Eden from the frozen grip of cherubim
         if Joshua could still the sun
tumbling ash freeze Herculaneum
and glaciers petrify sappy pines,
I'd ask God to immortalize this hour
         but etherized butterflies escape glass
and mounted sea-trophies snap back
for there's no keeping what can't be kept—
at night I pray redemption will come, not regret—

Luke and I drink, eat fresh-caught fish, and sleep,
accompanied by the everlasting sound of waves

Day Seventy-four

sunny skies. offshore wind. storm stirring waves
a hundred miles out becoming blessed surf, sublimely shaped.
the sea moves, the spirit sustains—wind and sea and *sun*
in confluence: evidence to surfers that God is good

I hadn't seen the pelagic waters roll until they neared the cay,
where they $^{\text{rise up}}$ in thalassic rush a hundred yards out,
kicking up at the reef, breaking right and left in a serene northwest—
I ride the crests all day until the wind dies with the $_{\text{going-down}}$ *sun*

the dolphins I know join me at sunset in the $_{\text{dying-down}}$ ocean
they know me and my canine companion, Luke—
we all linger with each other as they ^{emerge} and $_{\text{submerge}}$
swimming around us, dallying, playing in the surf

the evening steals the *light* from day and gradually goes into hiding—
first **crepuscule,** then **gloam,** then **negritude** overtaking any glow.
I stumble in **darkness,** overcome by star-lessness and m()()n-lessness—
there's nothing in the sky but **blackness, obscurity, and fulginosity**—
I can't see a few feet before me—only the *white* of breaking waves
lights the **night,** only the memory of where to step keeps me straight
as I feel my way through wind heaving and blowing on the ocean

Day Seventy-five

solid **black**, a sheet wrapped across God's face
      slowly splits, as sea s e p a r a t e s from sky,
 as *light* rips away **darkness**, unpeeling it, diminishing it
      to what it isn't, transforming all the ^{hung} clouds
to *brilliant* coral as the band broadens, *illumines,*
      plumes, penetrates the sky with flare more salmon
than heaven—as all comes alive with *light*—
      my face, my spirit, the azure lure behind mauve clouds,
the gulls circling, cawing, clutching the sea-breeze
      the dolphins I know purling a *lighter* sea, sucking *light* air—
and all this as earth rises and I paddle out to waves!

Day Seventy-six

while the dolphins I know glide glacis with the grace
        of those who've lived ocean as long as sea
and pelicans scoot down pearlingBreaks
        with wings e x t e n d e d into cherubim
I push my body into morningWake
        and ride the sea that rides the wind
all the while praying that none of this will end—
        the wildWind surging horizons,
the bold *sun* pushing blue into the sky,
        the sea air whipping through my hair—
as I steer my board and paddle the crests.

"o wind and windRider, you spirit the wave
like a pelican whose wings never touch water—
you are *sun* that stirs weather, waveMaker,
        you are the brave who breaks waves and takes waves
fierce and fat," as I lay flat, so much smaller than water,
        so much thinner than the tall wind,
and wait for yet another swell.

when the sea leaps, my spirit leaps, his shape leaps into my feet
        as we catch the translucent swell and flash down the line
glassing before us, transparent as God, smooth as *light,*
        and breaks behind us into a million ghosts leaping into white
as quickly as they die—while I in that quickened rush
        of wind-catching-sea and water-chasing-water
"feel you, windRider, surfing from *sun* to m()()n with me."

Luke and I are desperate for water, having nothing to drink for two days!
        thirst is a horrible longing—the wanting of liquid
to satisfy the craving of the spirit and gratify the body's dryness

Day Seventy-seven

storm at sea!—thunder, lightning, torrents of rain!
my whole world is liquid, my universe is God
_{falling} from heaven—as the waves rise ferocious,
sounding like jets in full-throttle taking off!
the sky opens apocalyptic—the rain keeps dropping,
thunderbolts strike the beach, a downpour descends!
the entire firmament comes _{down} upon my head!
I hide under the lean-two with Luke by my side
trying to shield ourselves from the relentless flood!
the *sun* doesn't shine again until the end of the day.

Luke and I drink and drink our fill of water in the boat,
then walk, fish, and stroll in the breaking waves.

Day Seventy-eight

old **darkness** hoBbleS the coast
bEnt **blackness** woBbleS on the sea
hard cold, **strong** as death,
lies prostrate on the beach
everylivingthing is waiting for *the sun*
to be a miracle, a heavenly sign,
like Jesus healing the lame and blind
and me whose body is in excruciating pain

but the frozen sky numbs the sun
the open ocean is **cold Viking dark**
stallion waves *invade* the shore
and sack the monastery of my mind

the silver sea barely breaks
under sluggish sky with vacant m()()n—
pelicans flew away yesterday
the dolphins porpoised south

only a sliver of s l o w *sun*
c r a w l s on the western horizon
then is swallowed—
in a strange absence of presence

thankfully, in the evening it rains—
not much but enough to sustain

Day Seventy-nine

wave after wave *runs* and _{falls} forward
plunging *headlong*, breaking into elegies

I swear I hear the manacles
clanging of bent Africans

smooth silver tubes roll into lacey froth
peaks thrust headlong over _{deep troughs}

one martyr after another spills

slanted waves, clouds, and *sun*
slideSidewaysInSouthernWinds

freed spirits slip through the cracks of dawn

under jaded heaven *glittering* with diamonds
and chrome m()()n suspended by some invisible palm
the sea heaves and sighs, weeps and cries—
many are the suicides that happened _{under} ^{these skies}
I see them in COLLapsing waves
I count their deaths in crushing breakers
and consider joining them in _{deep} waters
because I see _{the falling sun} blazing—
melting a white hole in the horizon
and spirits speeding through the opening—
but then I look at my companion, Luke,
and wouldn't want to leave him

Day Eighty

contused sky smitten with piercing *sun*
bleeds into the l o n g t h i n h o r i z o n
clouds break, seabirds b e n d in breaking wind
as a sudden rainburst hides (half a rainbow
and I am soaked in broken promises

then I feel the warmth of the coming sun
because jaguars have fought night-spirits and won

in the evening I hear slow obscure ghosts
^{hovering above} me in the blind sky.
I smell the pungent _{uprooted} ocean,
as wind turns over _{deep} sea,
and as waves **dark** as m()()nlessness
spill on rocks and rush over my feet

*I stumble over **blackness** as I grope*
my way to the edge of my existence.

Day Eighty-one

while phantasmic fog **smothers** the *sun*
stallion seasounds surround my surfboard
and pungent ocean fills my nostrils with God
who breathes living *pneuma* into my spirit—
I'm alive in divine revelation
seeking truth in the beauty of waves
over which a moving line of pelicans glide
wings o u t s t r e t c h e d catching *spindrift* ^{upward} drafts—
soon the fog disappears like a *vanishing ghost*

on shore blackbirds appear
out of nowhere near imagination
searching for miracles in the sallying froth
as the sea ^{Rises Swells and Surges}
and *spills* on shore jostling shattered shells—
soon they will be strewn sand covering the beach
as numerous as the jagged stars I hope to reach

Day Eighty-two

dawn!—the ^{resurrection} of *sun and light!*
I walk the littoral in God's glorious sunshine!
as far as I can see—the e n d l e s s n e s s of sea—
if I were to paddle _{deeper and deeper,}
the horizon would move farther and farther—
there is no end to ocean, *sun*, wind, and Spirit God.
as long as the Divine mingles with earth, eternity is now

I hold onto Lord-Spirit as long as death doesn't matter—
trying to grip the long thin line of the round horizon,
living on promises as sure as the ^{rising} tide-flow,
having nowhere to go but into the dusk of presence,
_{falling} like the *sun* in the afterglow of my existence.

Day Eighty-three

dead **night** lies **heavy** on the horizon like a corpse
stygian sky is scarred with stars
crucifix clouds are nailed to the firmament
while the breathless sea is shrouded in **tenebrosity**

then an orange band like a loin cloth
wraps tightly around the wounded earth
as the sun *bleeds* into the eastern horizon
(rays s l o w l y seeping out of the coffin)
amber transforming into crimson
crimson into deep red and mauve
and mauve into purple ascension—
I see the dolphins I know rising
out of the sea dripping luminaires
and seabirds orbiting overhead—wings flashing

the fire of the *sun* is extinguished
as it dips into the western horizon
silver breeze rustles the palm fronds
full m()()n ascends the eastern ocean
casting a golden aisle of light—
Luke and I wade into the shallows
stepping into this cast of light
then I dive headfirst into the sea
fully immersed in evening glory

this night Luke and I drink
the last of our water—
I pray for rain from the Creator
I pray that my leg will quickly heal

Day Eighty-four

pelagic and thalassic waters, rough and choppy,
thrash, wriggle, twist, toss, pitch, foam—
the sea is rampant, turbulent—a *wild* being
with *wild* waves in a wet wilderness
rushing to shore as wildebeests stampeding—
the animal-ocean seizing the slim beach,
crazy white foam everywhere, billowing,
crashing, fomenting, surging, splashing—
I cannot walk the shore without getting soaked
but I am so stoked to join the savage surf,
ride the breaks as if they were bucking broncos,
and make it to the beach without falling off.
Luke and I paddle out, but the sea has too much wind,
so we give up, knowing (for the day) the ocean wins!—
but we win, too, because God sends glorious rain!

Day Eighty-five

as the ^{rising} *sun* opens the sky over the sea,
can I see the edges of moving space?
if I could pin the infinite end
I'd compass the way in *swift* stroke,
but nothing I know is *perfect/straight/round*
like *sense/sound/light*, it curves and bends—
even the runnings on my palms fall off the edge
just like the _{falling} *sun* TIPping over the horizon

the day turns to evening hues,
a subdued roseate coloration,
a palette of reds, pinks, and yellows
smeared on the dying sky—
as the *sun* _{falls} into oblivion
and the *light* of day dissolves
into the **darkness of night**—
snuffed out like a cathedral candle—
all is as quiet as God, as silent
as the Spirit in the **gloaming night**,
where *light* is as precious
as the nimbus m()()n and glowing stars

Day Eighty-six

the sun streaming, the sea flowing, the waves breaking—
living creation is enough for me to want to keep living—
I love the light, and enjoy the present-Spirit-Jesus-Christ.
feeling the spirited ocean wind, I chant as I stroll the shore:
Iesous, Pneuma-Theos (Jesus, Spirit-God)
Didaskalos, Rabonni, Huios Anthropou (Teacher, Rabbi, Son of Man)
Nazaraios, Tekton, Huios Dauid (Nazarene, Carpenter/Builder, Son of David)
Thaumasiotatos, Therapon, Iatros (Thaumaturgist, Therapist/Healer, Physician)
Huios Theou, Christos, Parakletos (Son of God, Christ, Paraclete)
Ktistes, Apaugasma, Charakter (Creator, Radiant One, Express Image)
Pantokrator Soter Kurios (Almighty Savior/Deliverer Lord)
Logos, Eikon Theou, Prototokos (Logos, Image of God, Premier).

the waves rise and fall, over and over, breaking into white water
surging toward the coast, rushing to shore, crumbling into fizz—
I paddle my surfboard into the beachcombers followed by Luke.
when I get to the reef, I get off, help Luke up, and give him a shove—
he rides the wave, gliding, coasting, surfing on all fours!

Day Eighty-seven

I have gotten so close and felt—
a palm blown by the wind. I waver
somewhere between faith and the next.
a cenotaph is not enough for me.
I hold the mystic spirit, but can't contain—
it spills and flows into water like wind.

^{raised} from the dead, they said—^{taken up}.
all the sagging rows of crosses, all the mute
monuments await the word. but there is never
enough wind to sweep away the tired from earth.
if he were not gone to ghost, oh spirit,
I'd have nothing but promise to hold.

they preach, they teach, they prophecy.
mouths move mightily, songs ^{ascend} **gloom.**
they dance, transcend, shout hallelujah.
chew Eucharist with humble teeth, eat host
and pray he stays them another day.

his spirit is enough of, the presence of,
the sense of, another, immortal, different
than ourselves, who's gone some distance
yet not left us hopelessly groping to find.
the palpable face *flashes* in the waves. grasp grace
and cling. I squeeze divinity as it passes.

again, Luke and I have come to the end of our water
so I desperately pray for rain from the Creator.

Day Eighty-eight

a serene cerulean ocean this glorious morning—
perfect for snorkeling at the reef, perfect for spear-fishing—
Luke and I paddle out to the cay full of expectancy
of fresh catch to feed us (by grace) our daily bread—
it all depends on my agility and my accuracy.
I spear one fish, then another one, put them in my bag,
paddle back to shore with Luke, and cook them both.
we have a breakfast of fresh fish, while we enjoy
the calm ocean waves lapping lightly on the shore.

I have looked for the *Parousia* to come on this earth,
but found nothing but disappointment and despair—
the coming of Christ Jesus delayed and delayed—
I think I'll look for the rain to keep falling each day
and not expect anything but grace to sustain.

Day Eighty-nine

Sunlight, pierce my bones.
deep *sunlight* heal.

I am wonderfully made?
then why unWonderfullyUnMakeMe?

I keep seeking *sunlight*
somewhere, kinder entropy

ending is a natural consequence
of your choice to make matter—
and to make matters worse
you give intimations beyond bone and lips

unless this eternity in my heart is Not—
but if I'm not mistaken
when I come undone
I will run out of body

exit flesh before I wreck: there's an idea
too Old
or earth a stint that *thins* flesh
until it becomes pervious—
excarnate in preliminary lams
going Zoa-winged. Angel it. Almost.
each dally rush waveIntoWater
escape flame from *sunfire*
Unbody part after part

I have too much knowledge: it Hurts

aching for *sunlight* to melt
thirsting for a psalm

into your watery palms
I pour

drink me in
Kindly,
Lord!

send rain!

Day Ninety

no, none of us
have ichor
flowing
in our veins
it's just blood
mixed with water—
and we are water
more than blood.
we deliquesce
in measures
some dripping
quicker than others
some seeming
not to evanesce
but we all do,
like a clepsydra.

while I argue
of fairness
and unfairness,
substance
trickles out—
something heavier
than me stealing
my best.
strange that
I can't hold back.
stranger that I
almost want
the drops to end
and the trial
stop without
any solution.

this evening—
thank God—
rain comes.

Luke and I
drink and drink!

Day Ninety-one

just as Jesus walked along Galilee's Sea
so has he moved among the palm trees
surrounding my air and face—
this is my epiphany

slim thoughts ^{climb} trees to see him pass
old suspicions fish oceans to watch him rise

just as Jesus flung love like seeds
spread kingdoms with flocks of words
broke religions with hammer and head—
so I fling, spread, break

Day Ninety-two

the wind speaks Spirit, the ocean claps,
the wide sky *suns* the sea-swept beach
all around me the Divine waves and shines—
I'm anointed by lavishing liquid God
who is, who was, and who is still to come
I'm surrounded by nature's sensuous sacredness
I pray to the Spirit swirling in the four winds—
Boreas, Notus, Eurus, Zephyrous—
God who is coming is Spirit who has come.
the seven roaming eyes of the seven Spirits
sent forth into all the earth
search for those who find truth in beauty—
how cool to watch the pelicans [sky-surf] the waves
and to swim with the dolphins I know *gliding* the ocean
as the four living *zoa* watch all creation.

Day Ninety-three

I see an orange rind wrapped 'round the horizon
slowly peeled back by an invisible thumb
revealing the fruit—the rising sun!
flinging fingers of *light* into the sky

the sea *shines*, the sky flows
pelicans soar, dive, and swallow
seagulls circle, caw, clutch the air
the dolphins I know dive, surface, swim in tandem

a falcon swoops and seizes a jack in its talons,
methuselah monarchs pass, flying to Mexican mountains
making me ever more certain
that Jesus became spirit in resurrection

Day Ninety-four

like a spirit possessing body and soul
a fierce rain-storm *seizes* the sea
making her tremble, turn over, and wail—
my pain is more turbulent than I can tell
I'm _{falling} a p a r t like the crumbling waves
spilling over, crashing, rushing to shore
the last roller will be the first to get me there
because the final wave is just the beginning—
the Spirit who is, who was, who is to come,
is the Almighty Creator who has no end . . . .

I watch eight pelicans *glide* the spirited wind—
if I had wings I'd follow them
to a paradise just beyond dusk's horizon
where the *sun* slides _{down} into gloom

Luke and I feast on the fish we caught
and gladly drink the water collected in my boat

Day Ninety-five

daybreak reveals *light bright* as transfigured Christ
who showed his divine face in *glory* as great as God

I have befriended death; she is no longer an enemy
I swim with her into the portal of the spirit of the sea

I am already riding the wave that is, was, and will be
as I taste broken grace poured out like wine

the dead *sun* _{descends} into dismal darkness
smearing the _{falling} sky blood-red

everywhere in the sky and sea is God,
the revealer of the Spirit Lord

Day Ninety-six

I chant in unison with the rising and falling waves:
"Iesous (Jesus), Pneuma (Spirit), Theos (God);
Christos (Christ), Pneuma (Spirit), Kurios (Lord)"—
I pray to Jesus, Spirit-God; I call to Christ, Spirit-Lord
in cadence with the three waves that break in every set.

the warm *sun* air feels so good on my face—
the ocean brimming and breaking on the shore—
I have found that beauty is truth, gloriousness is God!
I have come to the sea to see the Majesty of the Lord—
nothing that humans can do, can undo his pulchritude!
the waves still rise and shine, the ocean breeze still flows—
over and over again, elegant rollers bloom and burst
like flowers opening in the early morning ^{dawn}—
I have witnessed grace unfolding like an open scroll
which I have read ten thousand times in morning *light*—
the *quiet* breaking of sunrise, the *quick* breaking of ocean,
the waves unfolding revelation, the waves illumining God!
I cannot hold the apocalypse—it flows through my hands
like water surging, flowing, running, streaming, spiriting—
the Spirit of a moving God-in-the-moment emanating.
revelation is a now-in-an-instant flourishing of grace—
the opening of the glorious Spirit, the unveiling of God's face!

in my dreams I am taken away by the Spirit into an ethereal vision
of angels (cherubim and seraphim), *zoa*, and celestial beings—
as the heavens reveal these creatures to me in my sleep—
I see the spirit-wings of incorporeal beings. I feel divine entities
surrounding my face, baptizing my body, penetrating my soul—
I, like Isaiah, like Ezekiel, like Daniel, like John on Patmos Island,
see the heavens opened, see the adytum, see the glorious Holiness!
the empyrean is no further away than the words on my lips,
as I praise Spirit-Jesus for having risen from the abyss!

Day Ninety-seven

as the pains in my body increase,
Job-like I question; Jesus-like I plead.
the solemn Sovereign answers:
leviathan must devour the wildebeest;
behemoth must rule the sea,
where waves form, ^{rise}, and BreaK—
and suffering is no more than a memory.

I have seen a thousand dolphins;
I have felt a thousand *suns*
and seabirds ^{fly} my secrets beyond horizons.

whirlwinds *whip* the water into *whorls*;
cyclonic sea-winds *stir* and *swirl.*
tropical Atlantic is *wild animal,*
feral, fervent, crazy as hurricane-hell—
white-water madness frothing at the mouth—
no *sun* in sight, no stars at night,
the sky is sea, the sea is sky, mingled,
mangled, tangled **shades of darkness**—
my whole world is water, an enormous deluge,
I heave up the prayers of Noah and Jonah.

nothing is seen—not stars, not m()()n, not *dawning sun,*
only the bReaKing waves that turn *ghostly white* as they turn over—
the specters of alluvial *spills* on the littoral.
nothing is heard—not seagulls, not snowy egrets, not diving pelicans,
only the breaking waves that turn into drums as they turn over—
the percussion of the pounding surf.

*I hear the **darkness** of Great Spirit.*

Day Ninety-eight

nothing on earth could prepare me for seeing
the sea the first time—and ever since, I enjoy
ocean-heaven on earth, where the Spirit of God
mingles with the waves and the *sun* floods the beach—
water, rollers, and wind join together as one
to make the ever-living miracle called ocean

I surf the breakers as I feel miraculously one
with the ever-present-now-in-this-moment-God—
the wave takes me, saves me, thrusts me into "nowness"
the catch, the drop, the rush, the slide, the glide—
the cool sensation of moving-one-with-water-and-wind,
the elation of being united with nature's Supernatural

the day ends as it began—*sunlight* smeared across the horizon,
a palette of reds, yellows, and oranges spattered on the falling sky—
how picturesque is death—as attractive as earth's genesis—
telling us that we should die as we have lived—colorful, beautiful,
ethereal, pleasing, pulchritudinous, as pleasant as the sky at dusk

the firmament **darkens**, stars are veiled, rainclouds form,
drop precious liquid on the beach—some is collected in my boat

Day Ninety-nine

the sun ^{rises} **bold gold**, the sea *slithers* serpentine
as line after sleek line *surges* from the northeast—
a perfect day for catching perfect waves—
I paddle out and ride *again and again*
and then, all of a sudden, I'm struck!—
a reef shark takes a bite out of my dangling leg,
rips off some flesh and swims away
chased by the dolphins I have come to love

bleeding profusely (not again?!!) I paddle to shore
where I'm met by my golden retriever, Luke—
I make a tourniquet so I won't bleed out
and stitch the wound with needle and fishing line
screaming, moaning, groaning, calling on God!

all day long I lay in pain and agony
until the $_{\text{going-down}}$ bloody sun $_{\text{falls}}$—
night is more misery than I can tell—
Luke and I drink the precious water we have left
and I try to sleep but can't because of my pain

Day One Hundred

a wounded sun hoBbleS the horizon
b r o k e n clouds ^{hang} on the *imaginary line*
between pale green sea and azure sky—
I couldn't sleep the entire night—
the bleeding has stopped but not the pain

Luke, my dog, lies by my side—
since we have not eaten for two days
I coax her to catch ghost crabs—
he digs and digs and snags a big one
which he eats before he digs again—
Luke catches five which he eats alive

I apply antibiotic cream from my first-aid kit
and drink rainwater from my boat
until the sun _{falls down} dead again

Day One Hundred and One

the *sun* ^{rises} and so does my pain
but I must fish in order to sustain
(having not eaten in three days)—
I rig my fishing gear as best I can
and hoBblE into the shallows.
I catch four whitings, which I cook;
I eat two and give the other two to Luke

I mark the arc of the sun
as it reaches ^{zenith}, then _{descends}
and is doused like a fire
in the wet western horizon—

the colors of death are *beautiful*

Day One Hundred and Two

in the sedateness of my spirit
where anger doesn't roar and rage
I've heard the voice of the morning Lord
who speaks: "live more, live more"—
but my bleeding, aching body cries
and screams for its deliverance—
the Spirit sent from heaven's Son
gives me grace for perseverance

I watch a bloody m()()n ^{ascend} _{and descend} out of sight
but it doesn't take away my pain this night

Day One Hundred and Three

still in pain I wake to the *light* of the ^{rising} sun—
which is changing its face, transforming its demeanor.
as if in some kind of trance and some kind of spirit—
I am transported out of my body to heaven—
the *sun* turns into a glorious person, both majestic and meek—
she touches me with kindness and speaks to me strength—
in a flash my second soul passes through the *light to glory opening,*
to Majesty revealed, to the gathering of myriad angels
and beaming creatures roaming wild through paradise,
emerald green and translucent, verdant, festive, rejuvenated—
I see myriad faces, glowing with wonder, expressing delight
and pure joy of newly discovered divine contentment,
childlike, unjaded, unafraid—at first, I see faces I don't know
but the closer I get, the clearer they become—faces I recognize,
faces of my mother and father, faces of my friends,
the faces of my sons and lover, all fresher than ever.

Day One Hundred and Four

the days are long on the lonely beach alone—
thank God I have Luke and can spend the hours fishing,
meditating, walking, swimming, snorkeling—
I can do it, if Jesus could do it—forty days with nothing
but the wilderness, wild animals, and Satan harassing him

invisible God is as real as the wind surrounding my face—
as I trace the running of the waves onto the crooked beach
bringing grace upon grace to live—and more than endure!
I, too, have wild animals to face—in the sea and on the shore—
the dolphins I know; the whales, pelicans, seagulls; the fox I like,
and my golden retriever—my constant companion and dearest friend

Day One Hundred and Five

I hear the blowing of ocean zephyrs, stronger than death
and the ^{rising} of ocean waves, l o n g e r than imagination—
sky, *sun*, and sea rolling eternally—there is no end
to the almighty ocean traveling between the spheres.
I heard it all last night, whether consciously or not,
then I see what I dreamed—beachcombers, bReaKers,
unendingly rushing to shore, crashing on the littoral—
as I walk the beach with my dog, Luke, and admire
a rainbow spanning the vault and expanse of sky

the *sun* has drenched the earth all day, soaking it with *light*—
I, like a sponge, absorb *luminaires* until I'm infused with *luminosity,*
saturated with spirit, imbued with *illumination*, drenched with God—
and even though the **evening** is coming, I retain the *sun's glow*
deep _{down} in my soul and on my face, which the **darkness** can't erase

Day One Hundred and Six

I awake to *sun* and glorious breeze on the surf, and I realize
that each one of us is a wave of a journeying ocean,
a southern palm tree swaying in a sea of trees—
while Siddhartha Gautama still sits under a Bo tree,
Jesus-transfigured-in-spirit keeps walking on water—
he is the ultimate-only-on-his-feet-no-board-surfer.

I watch the *sun* ₍fall₎ in the western sky and the m()()n ascend.
I sleep and dream of tubular-barreling-pipeline-like-waves,
each wave shaping itself into a tube like a cave's entrance—
like the cave Jesus was born in, like the cave
from which Jesus resurrected and became Spirit,
like the cave Elijah rested in and Mohammed heard voices in—
caves are haunts of spirits, angels, and prophets—
I paddle into a wave-cave-entrance, ride the break,
exit the other side, coming out elated that I made it!
(but I pay the price—my stitched-up wound opens,
and the pain returns, as strong as at the beginning.
I re-stitch my wound, scream, and apply antibiotic cream.)

Day One Hundred and Seven

I watch the sea-surge in *sun* ^{rise} and sea-spill
on the littoral, as I hobble the beach with Luke—
everylivingthing-wild-and-sentient moves on shore—
I am overwhelmed and awed by the spirited ocean
where God is *light-life*, Spirit-effusion, grace poured
out on the coast, overshadowed by seabirds soaring—
I see their volant wings and I hear their morning cries.
today will be a good-God-day for fishing at the reef—
if I have enough strength—the pain in my leg from the shark-bite
and the stabbing pain in my back from the pancreatic cancer
want to hold me back—but I must move forward if we are to eat.
Luke and I paddle to the reef, where I snorkel and spear-fish.
I spear two wrasses, thanking God for life-giving death!

Day One Hundred and Eight

the morning clouds part like the Red Sea and reveal the *sun*
climbing from obscurity into the great wide-open sky—
I am washed in healing *sunlight* from Jesus, *iatros, therapon,*
(physician, healer)—his spiritual heat feels so good on my pains—
I can move, I can swim out to the reef to snorkel and fish.
I spear three angel fish (feeling guilty), but we have to live.
like the native Americans, I thank the fish for their sacrifice.
I, too, will die, so very soon, and give my body to the sea—
but I will live on in spirit, an endless wave, free from mortality!

Day One Hundred and Nine

the beach opens to a wide ocean breaking hard
with rollers slamming the reef and littoral—
Luke and I paddle out, gasping for breath,
as we are pummeled by tall waves, set after set.
Luke keeps his nostrils above the breaks.
I keep my surfboard floating above the wakes.
once we reach the calm near the cay,
I help Luke get on the board and push him forward—
he rides a beachcomber all the way to shore
with me hollering "ride it, Luke! ride it all the way!"
I bodysurf the next rolling wave to the beach,
grab my board, go out again, and ride a beautiful break!

we live the rest of the day, fishing, cleaning fish,
feasting, resting, walking the beach, admiring God
whose sunset is brilliant orange, vermillion, and red!

Day One Hundred and Ten

the rhythmic motion of the ocean—the tide,
the waves breaking on the littoral—syncopated,
falling heavy on the beach, then light, then heavy—
I can sing to the sea, with the sea's cadence and pulse,
breaking, throbbing, vibrating, thumping, stroking
the strand with billows, breakers, sets of waves.
I brave the ocean, with Luke paddling by my side,
anticipating rides in rising, rolling beachcombers—
Luke gets on the board and I shove him into a roll
which he rides, triumphantly, all the way to shore.
I retrieve the surfboard, paddle out, and ride a break
that takes me swiftly a hundred yards to my right!
God, the Infinite, All-Powerful Maker, is so good
to provide us beaming *sunlight* and drumming sea!

Day One Hundred and Eleven

how I love listening to the ^{sun rise}
as Holy Wind passes through everylivingthing
and every sentient being on the planet
breathes the same moving, living God!

I swim in the shallows and snorkel in the reef,
admiring the colorful tropical fish and glowing corrals,
wondering why their world is so susceptible to man,
who has the power to destroy and the power to sustain.

how I love listening to the _{sun set}
as Holy Wind circulates through everylivingthing
and every living creature, swimming, roaming, and flying,
breathes the same Spiritual Being.

Day One Hundred and Twelve

I smell pungent, uprooted sea reaching into my nostrils
I hear the seabirds cawing, singing, clacking, crying—
they fly in hundreds from inlet to inlet
searching for a morning meal of fresh fish
I, with my dog, wade into the breaking surf
with my longboard, anxious to surf waste-high breaks—
(Jesus is so good to me at my age)—I can still catch
the small beachcombers rolling over the sandbars
and ride them for all their worth into shore

I spend the rest of the day fishing for blues and spots
and having caught a lot, I share them with Luke—
we watch the day end as it began—sun streaking
on the horizon in blazing yellows and deep reds—
spreading *glory* from one island coast to the other

eventually a small storm arises in the west
and falls droplets on the beach and boat

Day One Hundred and Thirteen

the winds *speed* up and *siren* to shore
on the wheel, the round wheel
the wheel within the wheels
the eye within the round eyes
circling unconsciously
furiously flashing, pushing the clock
backward to heart-pounding **halt**
as the engine *speeds* past
as a sea-sucking tongued funnel
whirls fury on the island
with behemoth, cyclonic winds
relentless breakers rush the shore
like a stampede of wild horses
the *sun* is **obscured in tenebrous gloom**—
light is nowhere, **darkness** is everywhere
as thick as tightly packed grains of sand
I have no escape but to hide under the lean-two
with Luke trembling by my side

Day One Hundred and Fourteen

the heavens bend, break, and heave
as a *hurricane* twists the palms
and wings *wild* over the turbulent sea
whipping up waves as high as ten feet

rain-bursts everywhere turn land into ponds
and make rivers that *rush* into the ocean—
it's all part of the illimitable circling
of water falling, streaming, and flowing

and while the world is looking like Noah's flood
I spot a sea-hawk searching the sea for food—
she must have to feed a brood of young
to brave this *stormy, wind-whirling* cyclone—
tropical winds keep slamming the coast
waves riseRushCrashCrumble
stout sea-winds crush the shore—
a tempest *stirred* by the divine hand
who also, from the sea, *brought forth* dry land

Day One Hundred and Fifteen

an after-storm, cold northwest wind
flattens the sea like a corpse
death to seabirds and dolphins
numbness to my old digitals—
lump **darkness** weighs heavily on my bones—
but then the *sun*, Elijah-like,
lays its warm body _{down}
chest-to-chest, palm-to-palm, mouth-to-mouth
breathing warm pneuma into my lifelessness

the cold day transforms into colder night
as the *sunlight* becomes m()()nlight
and the one star *transforms into millions*
looking frozen in the **night** sky

Day One Hundred and Sixteen

slowly, stealthily, like a hunched tiger
morning light sneaks up on its prey,
darts, then pounces on **the darkness**
strangling its neck, suffocating its breath
bloodying the horizon sanguine—
my opaqueness is swallowed, weariness eaten.

I spend the day wading the sea and fishing
until the crescent m()()nlight ^rises^ on the ocean
and massive *star-shine* floods the sky—
the Milky Way is aglow with God!
I watch the surf ^ascend^, wave,
and splash pelicans coasting across the face—
I count the seabirds as they pass
and wonder how many days I have left
(thank God, Luke and I have plenty to drink!)

Day One Hundred and Seventeen

I dive into the tumultuous sea, tumble, and feel
the force that flows and circles in oceanic power—
I somersault again and again in the strong surf,
not knowing which way is up or down.
I thrust through deep, splattered sun-streaks,
and **darkness** turning me upside down.
I feel water shaking, falling, slapping.
I spurt, vibrate, rotate, circulate
like a wave within a wave within a wave
like a seabird gyrating in a whirlwind—
I keep tumbling in a cyma curve bending,
water rushing up my nose, filling my ears.
I turn over and over, tossed around like a seal
being played-with by a killer whale.
I hit my head on a sandbar, and die
for a few minutes, I guess—anyway, I'm not alive—
as I fall into the spirit world of pure light,
pure love, pure God, where everything is flowing—
like the ocean, like the wind, like *pneuma,*
and everything is floating down the river of life—
I feel complete freedom, lightness of being—
I look down from above and see myself tumbling,
rolling over and over in the breaking waves—
then I begin to see faces of my father, my wife,
my sons, my friends, my brothers—then suddenly I awake
to my heavy body being pummeled on the beach—
I gasp for breath, not knowing if I'm alive or dead.

as I crawl to the boat, Luke comes along side,
licking my wounds—I am bleeding everywhere—
my arms, my knees, my legs, my feet, and my head.

Day One Hundred and Eighteen

m()()nless heavens, *sunless* morning
_{falling} sky, crashing ocean
no seagulls cawing, no dolphins porpoising—
darkness soaks the beach—
I know I'm dying—
my strength falling like a waning tide

prostrating its thick hulk
darkness s t r e t c h e s across the horizon
under glaciated sky
cold waves *lean forward*
stars are canting a funerary dirge
planets, like Venus, cry in the sky
earth moans for murder and madness—
today, more elephants are shot for their tusks,
lions and leopards growl in their caged torture,
rhinos are killed for their horns, sharks de-finned,
humanity creates more carbon emissions,
and I am one hour closer
to the silence of the Creator

Day One Hundred and Nineteen

before *dawn*, full nimbus m()()n ^{floats} on the horizon
and Venus ^{hovers above} the eastern ocean—
otherwise, sad **darkness** broods in my soul
otherwise, spiritless **blackness** _{deepens} my hell
o sun! ^{rise} on pelican wings! *flash! fling!*
speed! ^{ascend! lift} my pain to heaven!

then I see soaring seabirds silhouette the ^{rising} *sun*
passing high overhead—shadows speeding on the sand—
the dolphins I know emerge in the *sea-sun-light*
and surf the gentle waves to the littoral.
struggling, I paddle out with Luke to join them.

I am freed for the rest of the day to wander like a ghost,
to wonder where I came from and where I will go.

suppressing my dolor, I walk the seaside after sunset,
until the m()()n and stars appear in the *brilliant Milky Way*—
and I have the distinct intimation that I am not alone—
other planets *circling* other stars could have seas as here
and some soul could be wandering an ocean, thinking what I am.

Luke and I eat some fresh fish I caught and drink our last water—
I pray again to the Creator, asking for mercy, asking for rain.

One Hundred and Twenty

wind on the ocean—*anemos thalassa*—
speaks God is Spirit—*theos pneuma.*
the *anemos* blows where it wills,
the *pnoe* stirs, blusters, gales, chills.
I have seen the Spirit as if it were a ghost—
God as Spirit, Jesus as Spirit, the Lord-Spirit
flowing through me as if I were a phantom.
I am receiving the divine *pneuma* breathing into me—
a rush of divinity, a wave of *theos*, a holy ghost of God.
nothing is more exhilarating than to ride a Spirit-wave—
in pneuma, anemos, pnoe (spirit, wind, breath).

One Hundred and Twenty-one

a brisk northwest wind flattens the sea—
perfect for snorkeling and spear-fishing—
I paddle out (with Luke nearby) to the reef,
dive under the water, which is only four feet deep,
and shoot my spear-gun at a barracuda—
I strike him, snag him, and bag him
(one of the biggest fish swimming the cay)—
we have fish to eat the whole day!

the rest of the morning and into the afternoon
I wander the beach and wonder about God
who, like the wind, is freeing Spirit, liberating Life,
Giver of grace, Revealer of light and splendor!
I glory in God as *sunlight* spreads upon the beach
and discover that God as Spirit is within my reach!

One Hundred and Twenty-two

the morning *sun* barely *shines* behind a sheen of clouds,
but a storm last night kicks up glorious chest-high waves—
we have rainwater! we have surf! Luke and I are stoked!
what could be better in our isolated world on this island?
Luke and I take turns surfing, then we go spear-fishing,
catching our breakfast, lunch, and dinner all at once!
I feel bad for the fish I speared at the reef—
I thank them for their sacrifice (from death comes life).

Day One Hundred and Twenty-three

the *sun* ^{emerges} from the soaked horizon
and lovely *ethereal* waves appear—
but *weak* as I am, I cannot surf
so I rehearse in my mind the best breakers
I have ridden from the deep to shore—
my first Pacific ride near San Francisco
in cold gray November rolling waters;
the long rights in San Diego at Scripps Beach,
La Jolla Shores, and sun-soaked Crystal Pier;
the hundreds of sweet arch-shaped rollers
in offshore winds in Costa Rica's Playa Guiones;
the multiple beautiful rights and flowing lefts
in warm December surf at Waimea Bay in Kauai;
my first fun catches in the Atlantic's Isle of Palms;
the memorable breakers at famed Frisco Beach
near the fishing pier at wind-whipped Cape Hatteras;
the thousands of beachcombers at my local surf,
the oldest seaside resort—Carolinian Pawleys Island;
and so many more waves that broke my way—
but today I have t*oo much pain* to enter the ocean again

bright day *transmogrifies* into **bleak** evening
as obscured sun _{descends} behind **dark** clouds
thankfully, I believe in the bright *parousia*—
the coming of majestic *Light*! *and I still hope*
death will be the surprise of everything

Day One Hundred and Twenty-four

sunless vapid morning
blackbird sheen covering ocean
abysmal **gloom** broods
as **umbra** obscures lucidity

dark spirits suffocate
opaque sky seals

black panther darkness
strangles the *sun*

suddenly! *sunbeams*!
breaking through the cumulous—
billows and rollers appear
as clouds and sea lope parallel

my journey is nearing its end
as the last beams of *sunlight*
are absorbed into the **hard** horizon—
a chrome half-m()()n ^{rises} on the other side
and zoic constellations crowd the heavens—
I ^{lift} my eyes and read the revelations

Day One Hundred and Twenty-five

I'm totTeRing on the edge of *sun*-spill
_{falling} headlong into foreverness—
I have very few days left to live—
the ache in my pancreas, back, and old bones
is too much to feel—I faint under the **weight.**
piles and piles of pain are thrown on me
in throe-after-throe, wave-after-wave—
relentless pounding of anguish and torture
unspeakable excruciation and throbbing affliction—
I am being crucified from within by nails of pain—
I watch the *sun* _{fall down} into a whorling **black** hole,
as heavy **darkness** and **opaqueness** suck
all *light* from the sky, swallowing everything—
thankfully I have water to drink, but nothing else

Day One Hundred and Twenty-six

the other side is too narrow to *squeeze* into
too big to flatten, too fluid to grasp
(angels *mingled* in wind, waves becoming froth)
I am too lost on this side to know
too fragile to face *Glory* head on
for fear I'll be squashed and ruined
and Love can't push me beyond

as my flesh wanes thin, the fatter eternity looks
the better I know myself and desperateness
for grace to come, *o Lord*, I moan, yet don't—
I am not ready, never worthy, never better

the new earth doesn't have days that end—
it is heaven, unexpected, gloriously green and new.
Jesus, the giver of all things good,
will wipe every tear from my eyes

Day One Hundred and Twenty-seven

my ears are drunk with ocean *spill*
incessant roar floods my hearing
as one wave after another percusses shore

eventually listening turns to seeing—
^{sunrise} *slanting* through sleek silver clouds
sunrays Sliding _{down} smooth mercurial waves

for the moment feeling the ocean wind
saves me from my agonizing pain

night creeps up, steals the *light* like a thief—
deep **darkness** turns into deeper **blackness**
I try to sleep but my agony cannot find Morpheus

Day One Hundred and Twenty-eight

sacred *sun shines* on the savannah sea—
the ocean is my wide wilderness,
where a mystic voice calls out to me:
"come, join the ancestral spirits of the living dead,
surf the waves with specters who don't want rest,
ride the sleek peaks, taking off on the crests."

I need a shaman to do a sacred dance for me,
a medicine man to ingest the holy peyote
and contact the other-worldly kachina-spirits
that can breathe healing into my being,
freeing me, body and soul, from the cancer—
will God hear my desperate prayer?
or am I destined, so very soon, to meet my Maker?

Day One Hundred and Twenty-nine

I have carried them in my spirit
(always my sons, always my sons)
the dolphins I know ^{porpoising} the sunlit sea
^{raise} their dorsals into ^{sun-dawn}
to suck air through their nostrums
(I hear them, I see them)

they have saved a thousand drownings
they are rescuing me this ocean morning

I have carried them in my heart
I have not let them drown in turgid depths
(always my sons, always my sons)
my wraith and exodus will come
and I will join the ^{winging} angels
but for today I feel *lighter*
as I watch the dolphins _{dive deeper}
until they vanish in sun-soaked waters

the sun _{drops,} *light* disappears, and its luster evanesces
as *twilight* turns into gloaming and gloaming turns into **darkness**
I am lost in Stygian murkiness, covered by Cimmerian **blackness**
unable to sleep, I await ^{sunrise} promise—
but, thank God, in the evening it rains and rains!

Day One Hundred and Thirty

I watch sky and sea part like lips
and **darkness** swallowed by *light*—
dawn mouths, sea leaps—sun throws,
daybreak dolphins—ocean porpoises—
cloud-rollers crush tide-rise—
waves beNd, break like *sunlight,*
hurl, curl, spill as spirit-specters
and ocean runs with seabird winds
as line after line of swift pelicans
surf updrafts of undulations
and I'm ready to spirit-soar
leaving this earth with my wraith
journeying beyond in my second soul

Day One Hundred and Thirty-one

I am leaving the *sunshine* for **Hades**
I am stepping by faith into the next—
where God's *glory* is the *light* in Jesus' face.
I'm excited that I will surf unfailing breaks.

the morning *breaks* into gladness
the ocean swerves and swims into the horizon
farther than I can see or trace.
I have found that truth is unsubstantial—
like the wind it varies to the east and west.

I trust liquid *flowing* in the ocean and in my veins—
water and blood are cousins, flowing from invisible God.

I've seen the Great Spirit push *sun* until it _{sets.}
I've seen the ^{soaring} sea-hawk's talons clutch a wriggling fish.
I've heard the wind ^{swirling over} the open waves.
I've heard God speaking on the *brighter* side of the grave.

Day One Hundred and Thirty-two

open ocean mystifying me—
dark wonders, deep mysteries swim in her.
open pelagic waters flowing to me—
sea swelling, bending, curling, hurling.
open thalassic waters calling me to join—
sea *rising, waving, cresting, crashing.*
the *sun* ^{dawns} in the unquiet ^{sky}—
brilliant colors shout, sing, and cry!

I paddle out with Luke, not to surf,
but to wait for our dolphin friends to come—
soon I spot their sliding silver dorsal fins
and then their nostrums emerging from the sea—
they have come to visit us, to play with us.
Luke loves to chase them, paddling furiously,
but he never catches—and they know he can't—
so the dolphins continue to circle us as in a dance.

this evening—thank the Creator—it rains and rains—
Luke and I drink and drink, being as thirsty as a desert.

Day One Hundred and Thirty-three

the sound of the *sun's* wind *swirls* around my head
the purple-colored clouds fly above me—
it is a day for catching breeze and throwing it all around,
a day of *sopping up light* like a sea-sponge

I sing to the ^{rising} *sun* a psalm:
"oh, ocean, come back to me as when I was young
ever stronger and brighter than before—
as waves of splendor on the primordial, oracular shore"

the *sun* ends in unspeakable pain
I am longing for all my days to cease—
realizing death is not a moment but a process

Day One Hundred and Thirty-four

I walk the ocean under slim new m()()n
until the *brilliant sun* breaks the horizon
overpowering all stellar and lunar *light*—
as **night** morphs and flies away
a flutter of monarchs flits past me
headed for the Mexico mountains—
knowing their destiny is predetermined

in my weakness I can barely breathe without feeling
severe pain in my back and even in my lungs—
I swoon, I faint, I fall asleep in the middle of the day—
in a dream I see a vision of the beginning of beginnings
where **darkness** and _{deep water} cover everything—
Creator speaks, *light shines*, and earth emerges;
living creatures with living souls of every kind appear—
dolphins ^{leaping} into the *bright sunshine*
sea-birds ^{winging} and ^{soaring} in the wind
four-footeds running primitive prairies and woods
two-leggeds roaming sleek ^{mountains} and beaches—
all is alive with Spirit God—Earth-maker and Sea-maker
who infuses the Spirit of life into everylivingthing
from *beaming* ^{sunrise} to *glowing* _{sunset}
from *dazzling* m()()n^{rise} to *dimming* m()()n-down

I awake from my revelry feeling better than before
and know I'm about to split this world in my spirit rising

Day One Hundred and Thirty-five

the *sun* ruPtuRes the sheath of the horizon
and spurts *light-beams* on the ocean—
the morning is an aperture for the living Spirit
as sea and sky swirl swiftly around the island—
I am encircled with morning moving mana—
the Spirit of God *revealing* to my spirit and mind
the *Light* of God that *brightens* the divine

a tall wind _{falls} **heavy** on the rolling ocean
waves ^{rise}, bend, bReaK, crush, crash, burst
into a million *luminaires* surging foam—
as the sea transforms into liquid leviathan
squirming, squiggling, curling its way to shore—
the Majesty of the moment overwhelming my pain

black sky smothers the western horizon
sunlessness sops the *light* out of day
then the heavens turn into m()()n and stars
as I walk in the **dark shadows** of palms

a full m()()n soon dominates the sky
pulling heavy on the ocean's tide—
the waves barely breaking in high water
moving as slowly as my ancient body
a quick, quiet rain pours down
on the beach and our boat
where we collect enough water
to keep us alive a few more days

Day One Hundred and Thirty-six

the ocean is rumpled by slight southern winds—
nothing to surf on, nothing to ride into shore—
still, I marvel at the spirit-in-*light*-on-wind-on-waves
God is alive! he enlivens creatures in the Spirit-Christ
he brings the living to the bright luminescence
enlightening all creation with *light* from heaven!
darkness, caves, cenotes, even the abyss cannot hide from him—
God's brightness is omnipresent! his *lucency* glows!
I cannot escape God's illumination no matter where I go.
I walk in the luminous *sunlight* with Luke by my side.
we stroll the beach looking for God to lighten the tide.

Day One Hundred and Thirty-seven

the *sun* is released from **Hades**' chains
where it has been held through the Stygian **night**
and *bursts* into morning-God-*glory.*
the ocean waves, the wind swirls, the coast ^{resurrects}
with *winging* seabirds and the *leaping* dolphins I know—
all around I see sea-life in the flora and fauna.
all around I see the hidden mysteries unveiled.
Light does that—the coming of *brightness* to the shades.

I grip the ungraspable, I hold the untouchable,
I grasp in my spirit the meaning of ^{resurrection.}
I will not die when my body gives up. My spirit will *fly*
in the wind of the ocean *whirling* into the horizon.

the *sun* throbs all day, pulsating beams of *light*
onto the globe where I trek and fish,
catching three flounders, which Luke and I eat—
the day concludes with sundown daubing the horizon
with crimson, vermilion, incarnadine, and maroon—
God painting an artistic picture, a flowing mural
of creative *light*, spirit, *elan vital,* sparkle, and soul.
I stand in awe of the colors bleeding into the horizon—
the moments of death are so spiritual!

Day One Hundred and Thirty-eight

the *rising* *sun* blasts the horizon
the waves *heave, curl, spill, splash*
the seabirds *wing* along the crests—
at last I catch a moment of meaning!

I watch the day live and die
as the *sun* rolls from horizon to horizon
and the sky unrolls mysteries in the clouds—
soon I will be spirit, soon I will be a wraith

I will join the myriads of specter-souls,
the plenitude of *pneumatic* phantoms
who've gone to ghost beyond the bones—
my friends, my lover, my father and mother

I await my exodus, as I drink the last of our water

Day One Hundred and Thirty-nine

the cold sky freezes my **shadow**
I bathe in morning *sunlight* trying to thaw
(my innermost bones crave the *heat*)
rise, Spirit Jesus, and breathe into my spirit
that I may sing, until I die, with the never-silent sea
psalms and hymns to the Almighty Sea-Maker

the waves are hyaline, liquid smooth
rolling softly on the shore
like butter spread on bread

these beachcombers do not break—
instead, they collapse on the littoral
crumbling gently—like tip-toeing white water
dissolving, like I will, silently into the sand

more waves flow and roll into sound
as the ocean oms its tantric mantra
ooommm-flow, ooommm-rise, ooommm-rush—
not a bodhisattva, I am reaching for nirvana

out of nowhere a nor'eastern blows in
and the waves begin to rage and roar—
the seagulls struggle against the wind
but I turn in the wind's direction,
make my arms volant and soar

Day One Hundred and Forty

the night, **black as print**, has stories to tell—
I read them in the designs of constellations

I feel unfinal, ^{hovering} like the m()()n
seeing everything flowing _{under} me

I see the *sun* balling the sky—
its *radiation* blinding my eyes,
which I open and shut
and see *glowing* spheres
black and *gloriously white*

sun-sea soars, color burns,
the surfer in me sees orange-peels
as waves slicing sideways, breaking light—

the breakers speak many voices
as the ocean calls the poet out of me

Day One Hundred and Forty-one

spirit zephyrs soar from the south
blustering gray clouds ride the gusts
over the ocean breaking from my right to left
in perfectly shaped surfers' waves
peeling down the lines along the crests

I wish I were as young as the *morning sun*
just now *breaking* on the thin horizon
but I am weak and broken down—
my blood, bones, and body are dying,
I'm fading like the austral waning m()()n

I see surfing spirits, gliding ghosts,
and phantasmic phantoms
refusing to leave the ocean, calling me to join

instead, Luke and I paddle to the reef,
where I spear-fish, and snag enough for us
to cook and eat—as we drink the last of our water

Day One Hundred and Forty-two

full m()()n, heavy with *light*, causes a King Tide,
and rain upon rain upon rain floods the island—
I'm worried that my boat will float out to sea,
so I hold on to it throughout the day, until I ache
so badly I can hardly hold the boat back anymore—
thankfully, the rain stops and I can relax.

I sleep, and have a dream, a revelatory vision,
I see the sacred Great One, eternal God,
who inspires the Watchers (sons of heaven),
coming with ten thousand of his sacred ones
to re-instate his majestic glory on earth
with peace, mercy, and forbearance,
with *light*, joy, peace, and salvation!
I hear him judge everyone who has defiled his Name—
the Lord of lords, God of gods, King of kings,
God of the ages, whose throne stands forever.

may his justice be preserved to all generations!

and in my vision I see cherubim on fire,
and thousands and thousands of spirits worshiping him.
then I am brought to a place of bright *light*
where the four winds whirl from the *sun*
and reveal Raphael, Uriel, Gabriel, and Michael
who are lords of the spirits of the souls of the dead—
they worship the Holy Great One, the glorious Lord,
the eternal King, as they surround the Tree of Life,
whose fragrance is divine, and fruit is eternal.

I see the portals of heaven opened,
where wind, rain, and mist flow to earth
like rivers of life proceeding from God's throne—
not as floods of judgment on the sins of men.
and I hear oceans of mercy and oceans of justice
flooding the beach where I am sleeping,
lulled by the ceaseless sound of breaking waves.

Day One Hundred and Forty-three

I wake with Luke and light a fire to keep us warm.
I make coffee, and watch the *sun* ^{rising} over the horizon.
I have given up hoping for the *Parousia* during my lifetime—
Christophany is already here. I hear it. I see it
in the *blowing* wind, *breaking* sun, and ^{rising} ocean.
I see Jesus-Spirit coming in the r o a m i n g clouds,
apocalypse revealed in the face of every wave,
where the ocean gives soul to our earth
and is the music of the Spirit.

Day One Hundred and Forty-four

inspired by peach-pink sky-rise
I write the ocean in watery ink
I write the waves as my poem
as ˢᵘⁿʳⁱˢᵉ *light* fully surrounds me
and the sea **heaves** *miracles* at my feet

scanning the rolling aqua ocean
I spot the circling pod of dolphins
ˡᵘⁿᵍⁱⁿᵍ and ˡᵉᵃᵖⁱⁿᵍ into *gleaming light*
excited by a fresh catch of reef fish
though weak, I paddle out to them

as I'm deep in the thalassic waters
I see two spouts even further out—
a mother whale with her calf
ᵉᵐᵉʳᵍⁱⁿᵍ then ₛᵤᵦₘₑᵣ𝓰ᵢₙ𝓰 as they head south
journeying an ancient, God-appointed route

all day the *sun* roars, spewing *luminaires,*
heating the earth and sea until after ₛᵤₙ𝒹ₒwₙ
when celestial bodies *light* the evening sky.
I am not lost in **darkness**, and I am not alone—
the lucency of heaven's nimbus m()()n
is my companion in the shadows of opacity—
I am able to wander the oceanside in **tenebrosity**

Day One Hundred and Forty-five

strong steady sea surges south
as southeasterly surf *slices and slides sideways*
steepens, suspends, sustains, spills, splashes
smattering the shore strewn with seashells—
small sea-stones slosh, swoosh, and swirl
as the swell sallies and is sucked back and forth

serene seagulls ^{soar} in the sea-wind
Spirit-sent in sirocco simoons—
slender skies s p l i t swiftly and silently
and *sunlight streaks* across sonorous seas
then dies in _{sundown} celebration—
the colors of blood streaking the horizon

Luke and I are parched, longing for water—
I pray for the mercy of our Creator

Day One Hundred and Forty-six

I walk, meditate, think of friends I still have
and those who have gone beyond the *sunlight*—
I chant for them: "*Iesous* (Jesus), *Pneuma* (Spirit), *theos* (God),
Soter (Savior), *kurios* (Lord), *Christos* (Christ)—
have mercy on their souls, transport their spirits to paradise!"

I continue to walk the beach and admire the pounding waves
slamming the shore, percussing the littoral, resounding in my ears—
I chant in rhythm: "Jesus, Spirit-God, Lord-Christ, Savior.
I need you Jesus-Spirit-God every day, every hour!
Be with me in life, be with me in death, bring me into paradise!"

Day One Hundred and Forty-seven

the *sun* is breaking, the sea is breaking,
I am breaking—the *sun* and sea will outlast me—
a broken man (the cancer having gotten the best of me)
I am filleted by the *sun*, crushed by sea's rush—
I am scoured by the violent powerful weather,
torn in two by the wind coming on the coast—
I hang in there as long as I can—I sing, I chant:
"*Iesous* (Jesus), *Pneuma* (Spirit), *Theos* (God)!
Soter (Savior), *Christos* (Christ), *Kurios* (Lord)!"

Luke, my dog, remains by my side, faithful as ever—
we have been through many surly storms together;
we have stayed with each other through violent gales,
stout downfalls, piercing lightning, and heaving hell!
Thank God the storm brings water to quell our thirst!

Day One Hundred and Forty-eight

full m()()n-beam dances on the sea
lighting the ^{crests} of the billows

one by one the stars unshine
eclipsed by the **bold** ^{rising} *sun*

the sky is *fire*, the sea is *glass*
as the ^{dawning sun} shoots *light-beams* my way

seabirds silhouette past the *bright* sky-ball
hallowed with nimbus red *radiation*

then a wild nor'eastern blows on the ocean
white-capped waves ^{pile} and _{plunge}

fantastic furious forces overwhelm—
I am spirit. I am wave. I am wind.

the _{falling} rain buries the ocean
like dust thrown on a casket

fog shrouds the island corpse
and I am as blind as death

I feel percussion *pulsing* in my blood
and read the semiosis of God

Day One Hundred and Forty-nine

orange *sun* b r e a k s the horizon
then gets **covered** in a mountain of clouds
until it ᴿⁱˢᵉˢ again *brilliantly* yellow
shining on the line of pelicans
gliding along the cresting waves
a multitude of seabirds follows—
seagulls, cormorants, and skimmers—
they *wing, dive, and ride* in the *sun-wind*

soon, so very soon, I, too, will wing

the *sun's rays* penetrate **thick** clouds
s t r e t c h i n g like mountains across the horizon
over which the Spirit ᴿⁱˢᵉˢ and sings like wind

Luke and I walk the beach watching seagulls glide
as zephyrous updrafts ˡⁱᶠᵗ them on ʰⁱᵍʰ

feeling weaker than I've ever been before
I s t r e t c h out my arms and pray Spirit God
to whisk me away in the evening breeze

Day One Hundred and Fifty

violent gale, blustery storm, rampaging ocean,
palm fronds bending in torrents of _{downfall—}
the sea is alive with whitecaps fomenting,
everywhere the sky and the beach is breaking.
my whole world is Noahic, deluging rain—
I am lost in God _{falling} from the sky.
I am immersed in Spirit-wind, Spirit-Jesus,
who pushed through turbulent waters in a storm
and came out walking on top of the waves!
I have no one else to save me from this cyclone!
Luke and I hide under the lean-two tied to my boat,
hoping we can hang on and don't have to float!

Day One Hundred and Fifty-one

blind ocean, hard *sun*, the sky crying fog
weeping for the planet's ruin
where has God gone?—
the Man, the Anthropocene Race,
has ravaged him—
driving spikes into his wrists
claiming he no longer exists

he hides behind a veil, a curtain of uncertainty
that only the ardent believers can penetrate—
Lord, I come at dusk to you through death

Day One Hundred and Fifty-two

Luke, your eyes, usually soft and serene,
can't hide your miserable pain
(how you've been such a wonderful companion!)
we surfed waves together, we ran the beach together—
and now you are riding that last wave
onto that long and distant shore—
soon, so very soon, I will run with you

I hold him until the last breath,
caressing his body, stroking his head—
believing he will breathe again
beyond this death, beyond this pain—
as he expires, his soul lifts, his spirit rises—
his palpable presence ascending to paradise!

I bury his body in the sand, weeping like rain
falling into the ocean from the broken-open heaven

Day One Hundred and Fifty-three

I can hardly sleep because of my grief for Luke.
I weep and weep until I have no more tears—
I miss my beloved companion, I ache for his demise—
there is nothing I could have done to prevent his death,
there is nothing I can do to bring him back!
but I will see him again very soon and we will run
eternal beaches and swim waves breaking on God's shores.

One Hundred and Fifty-four

resurrection! morning rises under brilliant sky!
the dead come to life—and I remember them one by one—
my multiple kin, canine friends, and human friends—
they ascend into glory as beaming spirits
into the panegyric gathering of celestial creatures—
where Jesus in Spirit appears in supernatural form—
as when he transformed Emmaus, the upper room,
the Galilean seaside, Jerusalem, and Olive Mount by his glory.

I see the *light illumine* the *wild*, w i d e ocean
blown by zephyr-winds into splendid sets
how I would love to dive into the water and surf!
but my legs refuse, my arms won't bend

I have reached my end, my sons—
my spirit is willing, but my flesh is weak

gather my bones and throw them into seabreeze
(they will turn into seabirds and fly away)
and come—don't hesitate—please come,
surf the waves that will always break

Day One Hundred and Fifty-five

I watch the *sun* rise from its nadir and travel to its zenith
carried on a palanquin of *zoa* rising from east to west—
the *glory* radiating the entire course, from the birth to death
of the *sun*, as it runs from brilliant sunrise to glorious sunset—
I watch *light* breaking on the ocean all day long,
the steady flow and glow of the *luminary* orb onto earth—
solar wind saturating the beach, the *pneumatic* God breathing
spirit into all his creation like metamorphosing worms into wings

Day One Hundred and Fifty-six

the breaking surf is talking God
the waves, her mellifluous poem,
the prophets speak in the oracular ocean
the breakers turn over in tongues—
the sensuous, curling sea, shaped like a god's body—
smoothly, softly, immaculately rolls to shore
where I am walking, deep in cantillating prayer
for my sons, for their sons, for my wife, and Luke
who has gone beyond into the Majestic Mystery

I drink the last of the rain-water that fell
a few days past, but I am too weak to fish—
I miss Luke and can't keep myself from crying

Day One Hundred and Fifty-seven

the morning clouds become glorious gods,
the waves become spiritual immortals,
running along the littoral, dancing on the beach—
who else but God can reveal his Spirit to the dying?

I have searched and searched and found no one.

the morning *sun* rises ^{higher}, as wind stirs the ocean.
I walk into the seabreeze coming from the north,
praying my exodus will be swift, but I know better—
the cancer has been eating away my flesh inch-by-inch.

I will rise thin as air like the pelicans I am watching now.

Day One Hundred and Fifty-eight

I watch the *sun* rise, zenith, and arc its way to sundown
the day lives, dies, and melts into the $_{falling}$ horizon—
I must pass through death, as every mortal creature does,
but it is not the end, as every holy man throughout the ages says—
what waits beyond is Great Mystery, which only a few prophets
have foreseen—such as Red Cloud, Isaiah, Siddhartha, Jesus, and John—
whether they call it Nirvana, Eternal Bliss, Heaven, or Paradise,
 it is as real as the wind passing through me as Spirit

Day One Hundred and Fifty-nine

dawn-struck pelicans silhouette the *sun*
as they fly in hundreds to the shore
and perch in l o n g   l i n e s along the ocean
spectating the northern swell—
eating God and drinking ocean air

as I limp along the wind-whipped beach
six volant pelicans ^{soar overhead}
and then I spot one dead
sprawled on the sand, wings o u t s t r e t c h e d
gone from one paradise to the next

bruised sun bleeds into a broken horizon
suffusing raGgeD clouds with *colors* of slaughter
crippled waves limp toward _{sunken} shore
seabirds beat *bent* wings in crushed wind
a cracked m()()n hoBblEs toward the west
in a wounded sky about to cRumBle
as my wraith appears, phantom of my second soul

Day One Hundred and Sixty

I awake and swoon, weak in body, but still alive in spirit—
the morning *breaks* into visions and visions
I see the *glory* of multiple transfigurations
where earthly beings are turned into heavenly zoa
circling the throne, glowing with God,
gleaming like resplendent spirit-lit creatures:
sea-beings swimming in the eternal ocean
aviaries soaring over the divine mountains
wild animals wandering in the celestial compass
immortal humans traversing the heavenly earth—
the miracle of mana inhabiting every being,
the marvel of Mystery inspiring all creation

Day One Hundred and Sixty-one

as the *sun* is ^{rising}, my breath is _{falling.}
I am as thirsty as a parched sand-dune.
I am so close to death, I can feel it my bones!
I am ready to pass from this life to the next—
like the *sun* ^{rising}, going to its zenith, and _{falling.}

I am running out of breath. I deeply thirst.
I watch the last wave ^{rise} and _{fall.}
I watch the sun _{rise} and _{fall.}

having not had water for four days,
I will die of thirst in a matter of hours—
(I need soma in my soma, or else)—
but then I remember the coconut I saw yesterday—
I crawl to get it, take my knife and puncture the shell;
there is milky juice inside, enough to keep my alive!
I, like a stranded islander and a dying desert dweller,
suck and suck the nut until there's no more juice left.

Day One Hundred and Sixty-two

as I walk the beach, I spot a waterspout—
a whirl-wind, sea-funnel, small typhoon—
appearing on the eastern horizon covering the *sun*
headed my way with a sudden _{downfall} of rain.
I don't seek cover because I'm so entranced
by its all-at-once-power-glory-beauty-force—
like living Spirit-God swirling out of the **dark** sky
and appearing suddenly in all his splendor to humanity—
I get soaked as the sea-funnel rushes by me—
wishing God had ^{caught me up} into heaven.

Day One Hundred and Sixty-three

I am so down that I barely know the *sun* ^{has risen}
I am as weak as a man just whipped and crucified
(Jesus, you were almost dead before you were nailed)
the *sun-light* is painful, the air is hard to suck—
my body is heavily weighing on my spirit
that wants to escape, that wants to fly like a monarch
over the ocean into the beloved blue sky—
only my thin skin is keeping me from e t e r n i t y . . .
I'm wriggling in anticipation of the next moment
waiting only for my cocoon to split open . . .

Day One Hundred and Sixty-four

I struggle down the beach with death on my mind—
the waiting—the aching—to be liberated from flesh and pain!
the whole creation groans for freedom from the mortal curse!—
the transformation of corruption and decay into immortality—
where spirit, instead of flesh, runs like wind on the waves!

I watch the sea turning over and over, changing from blue to white
as each wave rises, forms, peels, slides, dies, turns to foam—
the unfolding-glorious-and-tragic-story of each man's life—
we all, no matter how magnificent in our rise, Peter out in the end—
death is the heavy leveler, resurrection is the glorious elevator!

Day One Hundred and Sixty-five

I am barely breathing sea, feeling sky
as I watch **night** turn into *sun*
which slowly ^{rises} to its ^{zenith on high}

then I see the m()()n crossing the *sun's* face
as penumbra slides into **umbra**
and the *sun* is **totally eclipsed**

ah! the corona! radiating 'round the rim
a blazing halo of blue, red, yellow flames,
a molten glow spilling (*as I am*) over the brim!

Postscript

the ocean is alone, as it has always been,
waving, flowing, running, rolling
beachcomber, bReaKer, beachcomber, bReaKer—
God coming, God coming, God never gone

www.ingramcontent.com/pod-product-compliance
Lightning Source LLC
Chambersburg PA
CBHW021144090426
42740CB00008B/929